ANOTHER TIME

GROWING UP IN CLARE

Haymaking – thirsty work!

ANOTHER TIME

GROWING UP IN CLARE

COLETTE DINAN

MERCIER PRESS

MERCIER PRESS
Douglas Village, Cork
and
16 Hume Street, Dublin 2

Trade enquiries to COLUMBA MERCIER DISTRIBUTION,
55a Spruce Avenue, Stillorgan Industrial Park, Blackrock, Dublin

1 85635 404 0

10 9 8 7 6 5 4 3 2 1

DEDICATED TO
JAMES, BEN, ALANNAH, HANNAH AND EOIN
OUR BELOVED GRANDCHILDREN WHO KEEP US ON OUR TOES!

ACKNOWLEDGEMENTS
I would like to thank the following for the use of their photographs: Independent News-papers, *Irish Examiner*, Tom Kenny, Cyril McIntyre, Michael Rodgers, Jimmy Clune, Athlone Friary, Sheila and Paddy O'Dwyer, Nora and Maura Cunneen, Pádraig O'Callaghan, Leah Barrett, Geraldine Crowley, Vera O'Carroll, John Ryan, Jane McNamara, Bill Scanlon, Sheelagh, Ena and Seán. The drawings on pages 30 and 92 are by my niece Rachel Abraham.

Printed in Ireland by Colour Books Ltd.

Contents

A busy day in Scariff in the early 1950s

Those Were the Days

When I think about my young years, I naturally think of Scariff in the 1940s and 1950s – a charmed time and a magic place for all of us growing up there then. Our pastimes may now seem quite odd and very ordinary and boring to today's teenagers, but I can assure you we really knew how to enjoy ourselves. We had little or no pocket money. Pubs were male-dominated – indeed mostly frequented by older men. And singing pubs! They were something that just happened at the annual Fleadh Cheoil. Also, we didn't have the pressure of trying to live up to our peers. 'Peers' – we never heard the word back then. The fact that nobody had much in those days made everything a lot easier – and as for the latest fashions, well, most of what we had were hand-me-downs. Still, we didn't mind at all as many of our friends were similarly attired.

As I said, we had no money and yet we made our own entertainment and had memorable times with good friends and evenings of music and dance – at no cost. The main expense of the week was the Friday night céilí in the old parochial hall and the Sunday afternoon matinee at the Astor cinema. All this, believe it or not, for less than half a crown. Those were the days, indeed they were. Those far off childhood days – those halcyon days when time stood still – are the times we always recall and always will. Oh the dreams we dreamed and the plans we schemed – the world was our oyster or so it seemed.

Those were the days of cubbies and games, dolls, burnt toffee and pictures seen in the firelight flames. There was time for everyone and it seemed they had time for us too. There was none of the hurrying, none of the fuss, then. In the summer we read so many books, we swam in the mucky flaggers and in the evening, in Tomgraney, heard the rooks. We leaned on the bridge, talked, and discussed what we would do. Sometimes we sat on rocks in the river Graney and planned while the water gurgled and chuckled and swam in silver bubbles over our feet – and we ate our Dandy toffees. What a treat! We shared our girlish hopes, our fantasies and our fears, though fears were very few in those bygone lovely years. So many things can quickly take me back – a Mozart rondo, an old harmonium, a starry night, the smell of spices, a P. G. Wodehouse book. So many things it seems to set my heart alight and get me on a train of thought that takes me where I want to be and my beloved friends are there with me.

The hill of Scariff in the 1950s

Our one-penny treat

Cakes and Clover

My Mam made lovely gingerbread and apple and rhubarb tarts too, but in our early years gingerbread was her speciality. Her grandmother, with whom she lived for several years, taught her to make it and told her that it should be eaten hot to really enjoy it. Mam always gave it to us straight from the oven. The Cunneens, the Longs and ourselves would keep a vigil near the range and were always ready for hot gingerbread, tarts or indeed anything else that came our way.

Now, dropscones, a thick but mini version of the pancake, were a great favourite, and I was appointed chief dropscone-maker in our home. This job, mind you, had its compensations and one could always manage a few extra dropscones for oneself. I liked mine with a big dollop of butter. We had never heard the word cholesterol, but even if we had it would not have made any difference at all. The scones were as light as a feather and tasted sinfully delicious with melting butter running over chin and fingers.

Have you ever had colcannon on a wet miserable cold day? Food for the soul. Mind you, I haven't eaten it for awhile, and I don't know why because I've always loved it. It's amazing how important food is in our lives, not just to assuage our hunger, but for getting together with friends. I suppose we can mark out some of the milestones in our own lives by remembering some of the foods we had at the time.

For instance, our maternal grandmother sent us an iced cake for each of our birthdays. Oh the excitement. The cake, in a cardboard box, came in the evening and our friends and ourselves were always at the bus stop at least an hour before the bus was due. If by chance we had an old penny each we'd walk as far as Tomgraney, a little over a mile away, we would meet the bus there and ride back with the parcel – a sort of escort as it were for the last mile. The cake always arrived in perfect condition and was carefully packed and wedged in with chocolate, bulls eyes and butterscotch and also some special biscuits. Our Granny's present was like Christmas all over again. So, each of our birthdays was eagerly awaited.

Simple things pleased us too. We could make a meal of new potatoes and butter and never need meat and vegetables. In fact, the first week of each year's new potatoes was celebrated by making sure we had glasses of butter-

Busily clamping turf [in the late 1940s]

Letting the 'bellies' hang after tea in the bog!

Bogs are great – but can be dangerous!

milk to wash them down. Of course, the butter we ate with the potatoes was salted country butter – butter with the flavour of rich cream and with a lovely hint of clover … and then there was the bog!

In the bog, the kettle was settled on the fire and the tea was strong and tasted of smoke. Nevertheless we loved eating in the bog and the tea was part of it. Corned beef in the tin was the main fare. We removed each end of the tin with a special opener and pushed the large piece of cooked beef on to a bread board for easy slicing. It was eaten with nice grainy brown bread, and in between times we had minerals which were kept cool in the deep dark bog holes along with the porter for Dad and his helper. Well, I doubt if we were much help to Dad. Mind you, we could foot turf, but we were slow at the job and tended to wander off to eat wild raspberries and pick bog cotton. Dad always worried in case we might fall into a big bog hole, but thankfully this never happened. We looked on the bog as a magic place and at the end of the day we returned home on the borrowed donkey and car, tired out and happy, brown from the sun and turf, and ready for bed.

The raspberries, ripe and squishy, were there for the picking – sun-nurtured, unsprayed and full flavoured. When we went raspberry picking we always walked leisurely because we had the time; the time to commune with nature, the time to daydream and to chat lazily to one another. We had the time to be friends. We loved this ritual and I remember it well. It is a happy memory to be taken out occasionally and dusted, to lift the heart on dull days.

Occasions and Happiness

Wasn't it lovely to go barefoot and toss up dust from the sun-baked earth? The occasional stubbing of a toe was something to be ignored. Wasn't it great too to run about after summer rains and watch the mud squishing up between our toes, making muddy squiggles? What fun we had also trudging through the banks of lovely autumn leaves on the way to the October devotions – it was great! Remember how wonderful it was to trail around the shops when the windows were dressed for Christmas, tinsel and cotton wool making a dream setting for a child's vivid imagination? I think we always stood close together and discussed what we would like, though we always loved what we actually got.

I suppose it is a truism to say that life is what you make it – we loved life and we didn't waste a minute of it. We came from many different backgrounds and yet I'd imagine that academically we were much of a muchness. We were innovative, optimistic and fairly talented – and I suppose a little naive. But our naivete was never a hindrance – rather the reverse. We were fortunate that our elders and betters left us to ourselves, so we had the freedom to explore ideas. Also, living among those who were founder members of the Scariff Drama festival, we dreamed constantly of treading the boards. We were never idle or bored and we regularly put on plays in our garden sheds or back yards. And it wasn't only in our back yards that we starred, but on screen too. Fr J. J. Ryan, our parish priest, recorded any major occasion in our little town with his movie camera, and showed these movies 'without sound' in the old parochial hall during the winter months. Those evenings were well attended and we sat and viewed events from Holy Communion and Confirmation days to Show days and elections. Because of the many and varied subjects he showed, we were guaranteed enjoyment as we cheered and jeered the young and old alike who graced the screen. The first of his films were in black and white, but didn't suffer because of that; in fact I've often thought that the black and white had a certain something about them that gave them the edge over colour. When he moved on to colour films, we were always careful to dress with a 'bit of colour' in case we might be filmed. I know that if he were alive today he would be ready with a video camera for the free entertainment of all.

His recordings were not only visual; he derived great pleasure and enter-

Fr Ryan – caught on the other side of the camera!

tainment from recording conversations between children or the unwary. He hugely enjoyed playing back these gems – just when one least wanted them to be 'aired'!

Fr Ryan was a well-known, good Gregorian chanter and so we had one of the best amateur choirs that I have ever heard. In fact, the recording of the choir at his last Christmas Mass gives one an idea of the musical talent of the time, the love of singing he instilled in us, and many happy hours spent at rehearsals.

I remember too a very enjoyable concert during Fr Ryan's time with us. It was a musical comedy – in four acts – and was written by Maurice Kennedy who was then a teacher in the local vocational school. The concert ran for two nights and was one of the many things we attended and took part in. As a participant, one got in free. It was great! The hall was packed out on both nights too and I imagine it would have been well attended if it had run for a week. We had such fun that nobody noticed the cold; there was no electricity, of course, as it hadn't reached our village at the time, so central heating was unheard of except perhaps in books. The comedy, by the way, was called *Sing as we go* and was one of the happiest shows I have ever been in.

Then, of course, we had the travelling players such as De Gabriels. These

Our best show

PROGRAMME

"SING AS WE GO"

DRAMATIS PERSONÆ.

Mrs. McPherson (Hotel Proprietress)	Miss D. Moloney
Mike McCarthy (Farmer)	N. Ryan
Jim Cronin (Farmer)	D. Carroll
Mr. Lanigan (City Man)	M. Kennedy
Mrs. Lanigan (his Wife)	Miss M. Neville
Peggy (Waitress)	Miss M. Kelly
Col. Bumpkins (Ex. British Army)	D. O'Sullivan
Violet Jefferson (Film Star)	Miss D. Kelly
Bill McGuire (Agric. Instructor)	J. Ryan
Phil the Fluter (Street Musician)	J. J, Bugler
Danny (his Helper)	C. Treacy
Miss Kilmartin (Schoolteacher)	Miss M. Killeen
Miss Jenkins (Rich Old Lady)	Miss N. Hogan

School Girls (Dancing and Singing

N. Cunneen, M. Henehy, E. Henehy, M. Jones
O. Clune, C. O'Sullivan, P, Hallasey, A. Jordan
B, Treacy, D. Leonard, C, Long, M. Tighe,
A, Ryan, N. O'Brien, B, Corcoran, K, Hallasey,
J. Treacy

Recitation .—S. O'Sullivan

School Boys (Marching and Singing

R. Davis, M. Boyce, E. Long, R, Long, P, O'Brien
G. Jordan, P. Corcoran, H, Brady, T. Cunneen, M. Ryan

The Scene is laid in the Lounge of a Country Hotel
in Ballyscullion.

Accompanist : Mrs. C. O'Riordan
Written by : M. Kennedy
Producers : Rev. Frs. P. Ryan and G. Scanlan
Stage Manager : D. O'Sullivan

And now kind friends we say Adieu
And hope we've brought some fun to you
If you've enjoyed our Concert,—then
We'll hope to come to you again.

people were fondly welcomed each time as old friends and were well supported too. Not only did we support them, but we brought along our own chairs to the hall as well! Whenever any function that required extra seating took place in the hall, the people, well those in the town anyway, quite happily chalked their names under a few kitchen chairs and sent them down to the hall.

We never had to watch the clock before any performance as Mikey Dooley went around the town ringing a bell, letting us know it was time to get dressed up and almost curtain-up time. We were never disappointed either with the entertainment and though the repertoire of the travelling players was limited, we enjoyed and attended the same plays each year. Though we knew the plot we sat rooted with fear during *Murder in the Red Barn* and shamelessly weeping with the mother in *East Lynne*.

The travelling players endured much hardship and indeed lost out on a regular home life of their own. To us though, there was a certain glamour about them. I doubt if we could enjoy or even endure their lifestyle with all the travelling, cold halls and sometimes poor digs and very little money. Whenever I think about it, the past is a pleasant haze, drowsy with happy memories and occasional little worries and phobias. But I find that the happy times dominate and I suppose this isn't just forgetfulness, but the extrovert me burying what I do not wish to recollect. When I search back I would love to have clearer recall of certain things: the sound of my Dad's voice, for instance, will not come to mind though I can clearly call to memory the voices of neighbours who died long before him. But in my mind, I can still see his grey eyes full of love for us and remember the way he would listen and use his hands when he talked. Yes, indeed, he is not forgotten and someday I will recognise the voice – because of course, I will hear it again.

Do you remember, as I do, the feel of itchy chilblained feet meeting icy lino on a bitter winter's morning and hawing 'life' into large old pennies to press against the frosty masterpiece on the windowpane? Then there was the heart-thumping excitement on Christmas mornings, cold forgotten, searching through the gifts. The warm pleasure, indeed relief, to find that Santy had come once again is fixed in the mind, isn't it?

Can you ever forget the breath-catching smell of dozens of wellies, old raincoats, turf and chalk in the school cloak-room? Then there were the secrets we young girls loved to share – and our chats and plans. I loved the feeling of being tucked in at night and a sense of being protected and loved and I have never forgotten the thrill of holding a day-old chick in my palm.

Isn't it amazing how teenage years have somehow telescoped and memory of events is very scrappy? Still in my thoughts, the sweet taste of my first kiss – and the butterflies on my first date. The bliss of holding hands and talking, eyes reading each other, we felt, was our preserve alone. When I fell in love for the first time I thought that everything was perfect and that perhaps I looked beautiful. But, as you know, nothing compares to the sharing of marriage vows and learning to live with someone in close proximity – life is never quite the same again. However, the wonder and joy I felt at the births of our handsome son and lovely daughter, stay with me still.

I suppose whenever I think about the past, I remember it down a hazy tunnel – filled with love and quiet contentment.

The sweet taste of our first kiss

The Drama

'The Drama', as our festival of plays was called, was our annual excursion into the arts. It was a time of high excitement and we happily went along to many of the plays we had seen before. Most were repeated year after year, as is often the case in drama festivals. So, though we were very familiar with the story line of the well-known and loved plays, we would not miss seeing them through the eyes of the new producers and performers. We did not mind the queues and the crush – there were great queues in those days – all this only added to the enjoyment.

At an early age we learned to love the works of great writers, and indeed the not so great. Some first-class performers too trod the boards at the Astor with only us locals to appreciate their mastery, but appreciate them we did. We also loudly applauded the nervous newcomers unsure of themselves on stage; we were after all, you know, old hands. The work that was put into the presentation of the plays was staggering, often until two in the morning, whole evenings and nights given over to learning and discussing, producing and theorising.

In these days of television, videos and push-button entertainment it seems unbelievable that in the 1940s and 1950s we looked forward to the drama fes-

Scariff players in 'The Black Stranger'

The hard-working Drama Festival Committee [1951]

tival from the time the Christmas holidays were over. March was drama time and it marked for us the ending of a long winter. As I said, the standard of acting was very high indeed and the time given over to rehearsals was looked on as time well spent. I remember a 'Juno' in the Astor who to my mind far excelled the 'Juno' which I saw some years later in the famous Abbey theatre. Competing groups came to our town from all over Ireland because the Scariff festival had the name of being very well organised. Great fun too was had by all at the various venues after the performances. It was in Scariff that I first saw *Money Doesn't Matter, Gaslight, Shadow and Substance* and many others of that kind. Later on, we had John B. Keane's memorable *Many Young Men of Twenty* and his haunting *Sive*.

The plays, and all that went with them, seemed to hurry along the six weeks of Lent and helped us to stop thinking of food. Lent then was a strict regime, but indeed it didn't do us any harm at all – nor did we lose any weight either! It was very tempting at times though to raid our hoard of sweets, chocolate and biscuits which we were saving for Easter. My birthday, 21 March, boosted my collection as it were. We sometimes counted out what we had gathered between us, and I suppose it shows how steeped in religion and sacrifice we were that we could resist the goodies. To me, Good Friday always felt an unnaturally quiet day, broken only by singing in our choir the responses to accompany the Stations of the Cross.

Kathleen and Nora Wall, our next door neighbours, who were dressmakers, spent the day in prayer. So, of course, we did not hop in and out of their home as frequently as we would normally have visited.

'Sacred Heart of Jesus,' Kathleen prayed as she worked at her sewing. Lips moving, she prayed sometimes in a whisper, sometimes interiorly. 'Sacred Heart of Jesus I place all my trust in Thee' – and she did. She never doubted. 'Ask and you will receive,' she always said. She constantly prayed for all. For sister Nora who was ill, and for Eileen the nun; for her nieces, nephews and all of her friends. She prayed too for us her neighbours and for her many customers. When 'our' sad time came, we were glad to have her prayers because we could not pray then: 'For Guard O'Sullivan, may God take care of his soul and may the good God comfort his young wife and family'.

On Good Fridays she kept the silence between twelve and three o'clock while she prayed fervently on her knees.

'But why, Kathleen?' we often asked when we saw her like this.

'Because He has been so good to me, surely in return I should watch with Him,' she would answer.

All these years later I try still to watch with Him for Kathleen's sake – though I'm sure there is no need to pray for her soul. She has prayed her way into God's care. Hers was a simple trusting faith. Her God was a gentle, loving caring Father.

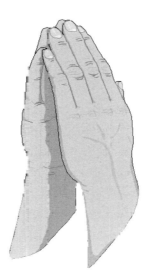

Sitting Out

Was it only in our town that almost everyone sat out of doors in the summer? Surely not! I cannot say though that I ever saw quite so much of it anywhere else. We brought out our favourite armchairs and stools to the footpath in front of our homes and we sat out there every evening in the warmer weather – the older people especially. We youngsters sat on the edge of the footpath with our bare feet on the road edge as we squished tar between our toes while we read or just talked. Neighbours chatted together, while some women knitted, sewed or crocheted and many of the menfolk read the paper or just dozed.

We loved the feel of soft tar and the smell of it too. We did not have to worry overmuch about bringing tar into the house. Carpets, you see, were few and far between, in our town. Lino was the main floor covering – except for kitchens and sculleries, which were for the most part, I suppose, left uncovered. Anyway we knew, you see, that butter removed tar quite easily and though money was scarce, butter was plentiful and inexpensive.

You'd have to be a brave stranger to walk through our town in our 'sitting out time' because you'd be well viewed, though kindly.

Sitting out of doors was a treat at any time, but when Michael O'Hehir gave one of his radio commentaries, the fortunate few who owned a wireless brought their set outside so that we could all be part of Croke Park on the day. We didn't mind what teams were playing, the broadcast always sounded so magical that we imagined we could actually see the ball – and the action.

We were fortunate that Kathleen and Nora owned a wireless, as it was called then, because we didn't get one ourselves until the electricity arrived in the town. Kathleen's wireless had a wet and a dry battery and occasionally was a bit temperamental. Still, we invited ourselves into their warm kitchen in the afternoons for the children's story read by P. J. O'Connor and we never ever missed *Around the fire*. But most of all I loved the comforting sound of the *Hospital Sweepstakes* signature tune 'Makes no difference where you are, you can wish upon a star'. And yes, I did feel then that anything at all was possible; that I would marry a handsome prince – and I did. Some of what I dreamed came true also and what a dreamer I was and still am to this very day.

First to 'sit out'!

Congratulations on a great win!

School Days

Cubby houses were the order of the day during our childhood. Each cubby house had its rooms marked out with stones – or had rooms beaten out in the tall grass, depending on the time of year. The cubbies were mainly in Mack's garden, which was second next-door to us. The garden was nicely sloped and was ideal for our cubby transport – an old-fashioned high pram which gave many years of service as a cubby taxi. Isn't it amazing how innovative one can be when young? We made cakes from mud and iced them beautifully with wet ashes, probably where I got an interest in and developed a liking for icing cakes!

Green nettle seed was a good-looking sugar too and the brown seed was coffee or tea – take your pick!

Cubbies and all that went with them gave way to reading novels. We read everything we could get our hands on – good or bad. When we had just about exhausted the book supply of family and friends, Mrs Boyce opened a lending library and it was a dream come true – for us girls anyway. Boyces was also the first ice-cream shop in Scariff, and wondering how we could earn the price of a 'pink lady' ice-cream, occupied a lot of our time. Not only did we get good value in ices, but we got good value at the Astor cinema too. The four-penny matinee was packed out each Sunday afternoon – well in the winter anyway. Indeed, ours was not just a passive role as viewers; we knew the names of the actors and actresses and the cowboy plots, though simple, had us cheering loudly for the good guys and shouting at the baddies. Indeed the matinee was a sort of babysitting service in a way because the younger members of the family were allowed in with the older brothers and sisters. So, I'd say the arrival in our town of the 'pictures' as we called them was a blessing for our parents and gave them the opportunity to read the Sunday papers in comfort.

We were a few minutes' stroll from the picture house, and we lived a short walk from the girls' and boys' national school. From about two years of age, I sat on our doorstep and interviewed the young children on their way to school. The 'bigger girls' as the girls from the sixth and seventh classes were called, often stopped to chat and joke with me too. I believe I looked very solemn with large brown eyes in a pale and freckled face, surrounded by a thick mane

Happy days – Scariff girls National School, 1954
[Note panes of glass broken or missing]

of hair – red hair at that! I enjoyed watching the world go by as it were from our doorstep and loved to talk to other children. I constantly thought about the fun I was missing and the wonderful time I could have if only I was allowed to go to school; God love me, wasn't I innocent?

I finally wore down my parents and they sent me off to school when the Easter holidays were over and just after my fourth birthday. Nancy Long, who became a nun, took me by the hand at my mother's request and brought me the short distance to school.

I believe my Mam missed her solemn but chatty daughter and made several trips in next door in the first hour and the three friends wondered how things were at school. Well, things were not so good at school; it was not at all the way I imagined it would be. Granted, everyone was very kind to me, but I missed my parents, my younger sister Sheelagh and most of all I missed Kathleen and Nora and the little snacks and small treats that usually made up my morning. I thought the small schoolroom was very drab, and the lessons, such as they were, did not appeal to me at all. However, I spotted that a child put up a hand from time to time and with a nod from teacher, they were allowed to leave.

Now, I was smart enough to put up my hand, leave the room, cross the road and run down the path. I sidled past our front door as I didn't want my Mam to see me, having pestered her for so long to get to school. I sloped in next door and, of course, I got a great welcome as I knew I would. Then Nora asked 'Colette, it's only half-past eleven, how did the teacher let you come home now?'

So, I told them the story and then we heard Mam walking in their hallway. I hid in their scullery. I can still hear the wonder in my mother's voice as she said 'Kathleen, can you ever believe that the lady stayed at school?'

Young hopefuls, 1923

Cock of the Walk

Looking at my cat stretching herself and sunbathing reminds me of pets we have had and one unusual pet – a cock called Bunty. He could be quite cross and very annoying at times and though most of our friends were slightly in awe of him he was a bit of a novelty just the same – and he knew it.

Several times when he had misbehaved, Dad threatened to wring his neck, but Bunty was two years old and as mischievous as ever when Dad died suddenly on a sunny 1 August 1954 while on Sunday duty at the garda barracks. It changed everything and our carefree life was gone.

Dad was a native of north Cork and a member of the gardaí from 1924. A farmer's son, he always sowed potatoes and many vegetables in the barrack garden so that we would have our own produce during winter and spring. We were glad to have all of this during that awful time following his death and when money was scarce for us, as it was then, the hens went in the cooking pot and Bunty did too!

'Is this Bunty?' Kathleen Corcoran enquired as she eyed with trepidation, the nicely roasted portion of chicken on her dinner plate. You see, as I said, Bunty went in the cooking pot too – because we were broke. But, when we sat around the dinner table with our invited young neighbour, we could not dismiss from our minds that we were about to eat our beloved pet. We thought of the many times our bare knees had been pecked by the same cock and I also called to mind how frequently he would run to meet me after school and fly on to my shoulder. We sat there for ages, hunger gone and sharing our different memories of the redoubtable Bunty.

Bunty – cock of the walk!

Dancing and Traditions

St Patrick's Day was a day off school then, as it is still. It was great entirely if it fell on either Friday or Monday and gave us a lovely long weekend away from school. There was always a small parade on the day, just after second Mass.

There was more excitement around then, in anticipation of the parade, than you would find on the streets of Dublin. Everyone, old and young, turned out for it, either to take part or to watch and encourage – but anyway to be there on the day. We dressed up in any green outfit we had and as far as I remember, we young ones wore white ankle socks too. I especially remember the socks because I was always frozen in them and yet we felt that they were stylish.

We must surely have come down with a chill in the following days because it was always cold on the day and frequently raining. Still, nothing would coax us to stay snug and warm in our knee-length wool socks. These were often hand-knitted and beautifully cosy. But, you do know the lengths we females – of any age – will go to for a bit of style!

Everyone had shamrock on a lapel and wore it proudly. Jimmy Wiley played the drums for the parade and he looked an imposing figure to us young ones. Tommy O'Donoghue played the smaller drums and played very well. We walked to Tomgraney and back and then were well ready for dinner and hungry enough to demolish a large amount of potatoes, bacon and cabbage. For a few years I was allowed to make the special dessert for the day and without a doubt it consisted of jelly and custard mainly. But greengage jelly was always used and with it either lemon jelly or cold custard and whipped cream. That made up the green, white and gold colours and very suitable for the day that was in it, we felt. In later years tinned peaches made the yellow (or gold) and a piece of pavlova, perhaps, for the white – such choices!

We always danced our Irish dances at home in the late afternoon and evening, though when we were older we were allowed to attend the céilí on our own on the night. J. J. Bugler could make the accordion talk, he certainly could make the most wonderful music and Billy Coyne's music was very sweet too.

I regret there was one dance I did not master – the hornpipe. However, my friend Carmel Long was a real expert at it and that was some comfort. Anyway,

I had my own version of the dance and I thought I was great. The four-hand reel was my best and four of us friends danced it with joy at any concert we were asked to be in.

A dancing teacher came to our school regularly to give dance classes. She was quite small, played the violin and cycled to our school from some miles away. I think our primary teacher enjoyed our dancing classes too, because it gave her a chance to relax by the fire while Miss Malone taught us our dances. I was always so big and tall for my age and she was so tiny that it did make me feel quite awkward, yet I loved to dance. As far as I know she was a good teacher – at least she did work hard at it. So, her teaching gave us a chance to show off on St Patrick's Day and we haven't forgotten any of those dances.

However, I'm more into ballroom dancing now, and a little Irish. We still celebrate the day in many ways and good food is a big part of it. But foremost, of course, is the singing in the choir of 'Hail Glorious St Patrick' at the special Mass. Later in the evening now, lots of dancing, and maybe a set – but certainly a Tango!

Do you know how to play 'The Mason's Apron'?

Easter Glow

Sometimes when Easter Sunday came it wasn't still quite warm enough for white ankle socks, but we wore them anyway. If Easter was late we sometimes wore a light twin-set and skirt going to Mass and probably shivered all the while. But if it was sunny and bright, we were determined to give it our best shot and dress up for the occasion – whether it was still cold, frosty weather or not.

On Good Friday, we wore our usual Sunday winter clothes, but Easter Sunday had to be celebrated in a very special way. It marked the coming out of the darkness of a lengthy winter and the prospect of a long warm summer right ahead of us. Then, of course, we always had more than a week's holiday from school and that in itself we felt was good reason for celebrating.

Yet, school wasn't too bad – in fact a lot of the time it was pleasant enough. Our principal teacher, Anna May loved literature and she taught us a love of

Happily going to school

poetry. She adored Irish and English poetry and many afternoons were given over to it. We stood in a semi-circle around the fire in the colder weather and stayed at our desks when it was warm. I got a few threepenny bits for knowing my poetry by rote – and threepence was a fortune then.

But to get back to Easter. This was a time when we began our country walks and planned our summer schedule – such as it was. Easter in its own way is a very heady time, isn't it?

Maybe we felt the excitement of the summer months coming up to meet us, because of all the sweets and chocolate we ate at Easter time. Or maybe not at all, maybe it's just something in the air at this time of year that gives a bounce to the step, a glow to the face and the warmth of spring in the heart!

Circus Antics

I remember when Fossett's circus took over the green and had their show there. The tent was small, or it must have been because it would not have fitted there otherwise. I have often heard my mother tell that one of the Fossett girls was born while the circus was in the centre of the town, perhaps this was their reason for siting the circus on the green. My memories of it are vague enough, but as our best friends lived right opposite the green, you can imagine the excitement we felt at this diversion.

The circus was usually held in Guilfoyles large field where the annual agricultural show happened also. The circus arrived at Guilfoyles very, very early in the morning and coming from the direction of Mountshannon, along the lower road below the town, and on to the field.

Our house, and the houses of our friends, backed onto the road below the town so we always heard the circus arrive, and it didn't matter how early this was either. I suppose there were such heavy trailers and caravans with the circus that we could not fail to hear it, especially when there were so few other vehicles around the place at the time.

It was a tight squeeze for us trying to look out the small open window of our back bedroom, but we did not want to miss a thing. I only recall lovely bright sunny mornings and colourful caravans – and no rain. Yet, I do know too that the entrance to the field was quite muddy occasionally, so it must have rained on some of the visits.

Duffy's and Fossett's were the only circuses that came to Scariff when we were young and they put on a great show each afternoon and evening during their stay. I loved the clowns, the performing dogs, the beautiful horses and the elephants. I never liked the high wire acts at all – in fact, I was terrified that they would fall and get killed. Yet, after a very enjoyable circus matinee, I was carefully and skilfully walking on top of the decorative curved iron which topped our yard wall. I was doing well – I had almost reached the shed and waited the applause of my friends, when Mam spotted me, banged on the kitchen window and shouted 'Colette, get down this very minute'. I did get down, I fell. I'm quite sure I would not have fallen if I hadn't got such a fright, but anyway the sprained ankle gave me a week off school!

I never tried that 'caper' again – as Mam called it. I still do not like to look at the high wire acts. *Terra firma* for me all the time, if possible. But I love the animals and the clowns. In fact, I would not need to have a big circus programme to entertain me, just give me good old-fashioned clowns, half a dozen horses and maybe an elephant or a lion, but definitely performing dogs! I will never forget the first time I saw a poodle in a frilly skirt, walking on her back legs and wheeling a doll's pram around the arena. To say I was enchanted is to put it mildly and though I've tried over the years to interest various dogs in pushing a doll's pram, they wouldn't respond at all. I have not given up on it yet though! The word 'circus' still gives me a frisson of excitement.

I remember how restlessly we sat at our wooden school desks, unheeding of our teachers on a 'circus day'. But then they too probably had their dreams, like ours, woven around bright caravans, glittering ladies and handsome bronzed men.

Do you remember how we kicked the sawdust beneath our feet while we listened to the big band sound and watched the antics of red-nosed clowns, dogs dancing and horses high-stepping? For that short time we felt part of it all.

Trick-acting

Gortmore was a happy place, and indeed a noisy place too, when everyone was home and neighbours were visiting for a game of cards or just a chat or a warm at the hearth. Fun and games were a huge part of the winter 'entertainment' there and trick-acting was greatly enjoyed. In a house such as theirs with three good-looking strong-willed girls, their handsome brother (my Dad) and their widowed father, you could believe that they played tricks on each other and on their visitors.

For instance, Dad went to a dance in Banteer one Sunday night and didn't tell them he was going out. Though he was barely seventeen he did not ask his father's permission either. The 'ladies' were furious when they discovered he had sneaked out without them and so they set about quietly setting a trap. Once their father was in bed, they tied two strings across the steps inside the porch leading from the front door. They then hung saucepans and a frying pan from the strings. It was not easy for them to stay awake, but they were determined and when he eventually returned home around two o'clock they were awake and listening. He carefully left his bike in front of the house in the shadow of the porch and he could not be heard opening or closing the door, so

Gortmore – we loved it!

quietly did he work. But when he took the first step up to the hallway, he fell across the strings and of course the huge clatter roused his father – and his father's temper.

Dad was grounded for a month and had to sit at home while his sisters went dancing. They were sorry to see him at home on his own and regretted what they had done and yet they often had a great laugh over it.

Nobody was spared, and if you ever felt a 'giggle' in the air you'd look twice at where you were about to sit and you would certainly throw back the bed clothes and do a 'check' before trying to settle down for sleep.

Young love

Chrissie and friends trick-acting outside Gortmore

Flowers and Flaggers

In May we always set up our May altar and transformed our bedrooms with all the wild flowers we could pick. We weren't too good though at replacing the flowers when they wilted. However, what's a few wilted flowers when your faith is so strong, you just know that Our Blessed Lady is really there presiding over your altar and listening to your fervent prayers!

We did not just collect wild flowers for our altar, but on every walk that we took during the summer. Once May was over the wild flowers were more usually placed on the kitchen window in a pretty jug. Primroses were and still are my very favourite wild flowers, they tasted well too – I remember how we loved to eat them. I would not care to eat anything like that now unless I was certain it hadn't been sprayed with chemicals or polluted with exhaust fumes!

We always sucked the purple clover and I can tell you that honey never tasted so well. We ate sorrel and all kinds of other leaves also. We were before our time, and did not realise that a lot of what we gathered and ate then would nowadays be picked to adorn special salads.

Our salads of long ago were very simple affairs. In fact, most of our meals were plain enough and I think we were all the better for that too. We sipped the white clover also, but did not think it was quite as good as the purple, though in reality it may have tasted the same – but the word was 'purple is best!'

On our meanders, we usually threaded the lovely daisies and made strings of necklaces for ourselves although we knew that they would surely be withered by the time we got home. But making daisy-chains was part of the summer and we were very given to tradition and enjoyed it hugely.

I always loved the sweet smell of the yellow gorse or furze as we called it. I didn't like to see it set on fire, but I could understand the need the farmers had to burn it as it tended to take over after a while.

We also collected cowslips, buttercups, celandine, cranesbill, foxgloves – we made thimbles of these. We made up bunches of dog roses and the lovely scented wild honeysuckle. We liked the different grasses too and adored the scent of meadow sweet. It wasn't just the fragrance either, we loved the plentiful clusters of creamy white flowers on strong stems that made the meadow sweet so special.

Confirmation girls, in front of the grotto in Scariff, getting ready for the May procession

The May altar 'dressed' for the procession

We were great ones for taking walks or I suppose I should say strolls or meanders. We certainly took our time and we had lots of it. We looked about us and admired all the flowers and grasses, weeds, hedges and trees. We watched out for all the hedge life so I can tell you our 'outings' were always interesting. We might only walk two miles, but we knew the two miles as well as we knew our own homes. We knew the very best places for different wild flowers, for the sweetest strawberries – and in time the juiciest blackberries. We knew where the birds' nests with baby birds were, though we never ever touched them. We knew where there should be frogs and the occasional hedgehog. And if you wanted soft dewy moss, we could quickly get the softest and the greenest. We were into nature in a big way without being aware of it and love of nature has stayed with most of us ever since.

During what we remember now as long hot summers, you could see dozens of us girls dressed in pink or blue knickers, cavorting in a place called the flaggers. Very few owned swimming suits and we didn't feel the need for them either. The young boys wore hurling or football shorts, if they had them. I cannot remember ever having such fun in the water. I am not really a 'water baby' as such, though the rest of the family love the water.

It was called the flaggers because for some reason, an area of the river Graney below the town, about the size of a large living-room, was covered in flagstones. Of course with all the swimming, diving and horsing around, the

Swimming in Scariff in 1947

Keeping cool in Mountshannon

Waiting for the 'chauffeur'

mud from between the flags quickly mixed with the water – but who cared? Not any of us!

Nor did we ever get a cold from sitting around in the wet clothes. We never picked up any germs from that same mud, in fact that muddy water gave us a great feeling of freedom, hours of fun each day and a glow that can come only from complete relaxation and happiness.

We were not allowed 'down the docks' as we called it, but it was near enough to the flaggers so we frequently wandered in that direction. We stayed safely away from the deep, deep water, but near enough to see what was happening. There was always a long boat unloading flour or timber barrels of porter and some quite good furniture came in this way too.

The waterways were very well used in those days and I wonder why the practice was ended. Can you just imagine the comfort there would be with this transport for any delivery of goods now that the roads are so choked with traffic?

The 'flaggers'

Picnics and Friends

Picking mushrooms was a great pastime and we never tired of collecting or eating them. We went searching too for apples, plums and damsons, but I do not remember any jam-making in our home. We ate the fruit fresh from the trees and our appetites were huge. At home, we cooked mushrooms daily when they were in season, and we sometimes made chutney too. The mushrooms were specially cooked on coals in an open fire.

Today, with some old friends, we had a big picnic in a spot where long ago we gathered mushrooms. Our picnic place was in Tobar na gCat and the sun and rain had helped to make a sweet scent from the hay. We sat there on the grass – squashing some lovely buttercups and daisies. The heady smell of clover filled the warm afternoon air and only bird song and our chatter broke the stillness. We talked and laughed about old times and some tears were shed too. But it was a very happy afternoon and it made us feel young again for a little while and contented with our lives and especially thankful to be together, enjoying the magic of friendship.

Setting out for a choir picnic

'Help yourself to sugar'

A memorable picnic

Night Noises

I never had any difficulty getting to sleep at night. In fact, I was often hard-pressed to stay awake while I said my short night prayers. We always said these prayers in bed in the wintertime especially, because we could become very cold indeed in a freezing bedroom – kneeling on lino. Once our candle was quenched, and Mam always check-ed on this, we were in bed until morning. But now and again and for no particular reason, I would be awake for maybe an hour after the prayers were said. The time awake always seemed very long as I lay listening to the night sounds. Invariably I would hear the soft scurrying of a mouse or mice up in the attic, and I always had a fear that maybe it was possible for one of these to easily come from the attic down into a bedroom. Then I would realise that if it had the temerity to ven-ture down, Mam's spring trap would be waiting with a bit of mouldy cheese.

One particular night I could hear Kathleen and Nora on their way to bed in the house next door. Both houses had been built at the same time and the wall between was thin enough. We were always glad of this and so were our neighbours. We loved the feeling of security knowing that we were all watch-ing out for each other. Before they retired for the night, I could hear their bat-tery radio – though faintly. I heard them quietly moving about, Nora in a back bedroom and Kathleen in the front, and when Kathleen coughed a few times I knew that she was settled in her bed.

I was aware too of the murmur of voices from our kitchen and was com-forted to hear this because I knew then that our Dad was in for the night – garda duty over for yet another day.

I could hear Alfie and Georgie going home through the bow-way, and the loud bang of a door. This I knew was Son Rodgers' back door; he was a quiet man and we liked him, but his back door wouldn't close without being banged. I could easily identify the steps as people hurried home. One more or less knew the habits of neighbours in a small town and it was easy to tell who had just gone by – we often made a game of this.

Now I can hear the half dozen or so men leaving May Coffey's pub across the road. They come slowly in the bow-way near us to collect their bicycles and continue their chats. These men are never drunk, they would not get the opportunity even if they wanted to drink for longer. May never served more than two drinks per person and if you arrived in her pub with the sign of drink on you, she would not serve you at all. Porter was what was usually served and drunk in her place. So, if these light drinkers had family at home waiting for them, the family could rest assured that they would be almost sober.

We loved to sit in the daytime on May's side counter that faced onto the green and to any action. The counter was a great vantage point and we often whiled away a wet afternoon – just chatting. We never bought treats there nor were we ever offered a mineral either, and of course we never had any spare money to spend on minerals. The only purchase I ever remember in May's shop was our weekly gallon of oil for the stove.

May was always called on if someone was ill or needed an injection. She had been a nurse, in America, in her younger years and a good nurse too. So, her opinion was always sought, before sending for a doctor was considered. She was an expert, as well, for making up rubs and potions.

Some noises at night always gave me a shiver – the creaking of the stairs when you knew for sure that nobody was walking on it. I lay there wide-eyed with fear, watching in the dark in case anyone might be framed in the open doorway with the landing window behind them. But more frightening still was the creaking of the bedroom floor when I knew that nobody should be walking on it. I could not switch on a light – no light to switch on!

I remember with a pounding heart, diving under the bed-clothes and pushing closer to Sheelagh who slept in the same bed. Then suddenly it was morning and nothing seemed scary. When electricity came those creaking sounds were not at all as frightening – and of course we were older too.

When I was much older still, I learned that the creaking sounds were just the old boards 'settling in' after the day – or whatever!

Baking and Outings

My very first attempt at making scones on my own was when I was in fifth class in primary school. I can still see those lovely scones – and taste them! The reaction when we heard that we would be allowed to bake was a mixture of excitement and trepidation. Many of us hadn't baked on our own before this, and even though our neighbours owned a pot oven, we didn't. I am left-handed and I had visions of dropping hot coals down on top of my scones, or buns, as they were known to us then. I had studied Nora and Kathleen working with the pot oven – Nora particularly as she did most of the cooking and baking. I was still a little worried. When Nora worked, it looked smooth and easy and she looked confident and in control. I did not feel too optimistic at all, especially because I had gathered from our teacher that she expected me to do quite well – I don't know why.

We carried the ingredients the short distance to school on baking day, and lessons were not very well attended to during the morning – too much on our minds.

I suppose it must have been a relief for our teacher when baking time arrived and the fire was glowing. We used two pot ovens between us and six of us baked. So, each person had the pot oven for the required time – about thirty minutes or so.

Learning to cook

I made ten scones and I'll have to tell you, they baked really beautifully and tasted just as they should. I loved the colour they baked – a softer shade than from our range and the texture seemed different too.

Carmel and myself were allowed to bake our scones only when everyone else had baked theirs and I suppose we were last because we lived almost beside the school. We walked home on air, very happy with our efforts. For my part, I was delighted that Dad was home on that particular afternoon because I wanted him to see those lovely buns – and praise them!

Not alone did he praise them, but he tied them in a clean tea cloth and hung the cloth from a hook in the kitchen ceiling – one of the spare hooks where our bacon was hung to cure. He tied them up like this because we didn't then own a wire cooling tray and the scones were piping hot from the oven. To be honest I would have loved them hot, but Mam thought it would be much better to keep them for our evening tea – which we did.

Nora and Kathleen got one each, of course, and I relished the praise.

We never had a school outing, but we had several choir and Legion of Mary outings or picnics. The outings were always to Holy Island near Mountshannon and because our Guardian Angels worked overtime, we always did the trip to the island and back very safely – thank God. The rowboats in which we travelled were always packed, very few children could swim and there was always a lot of pushing and shoving and manoeuvring for extra space. We invariably had brilliant fun and the late Fr J. J. Ryan who trained the choir, took much video film of the annual outing. I don't think we ever prayed on Holy Island – we had not gone there to pray you see. For the picnic, we had cake, sandwiches, lemonade and queen cakes and strong tea which had a faint taste of paraffin. Afterwards we had many games and, of course, a rousing sing-song.

Seán happily remembers a school outing to Tinerana in Ogonnelloe and to Killaloe. The main outing though was to the magnificent gardens at Tinerana. The house was occupied at the time and the gardeners took pride in their work and loved the plants, shrubs and fruit bushes. It was great to wander at will around these gardens, but that was not the only treat! Tinerana house had its own private pier and several boats. The school group were offered the use of the boats and encouraged to spend a few hours on the Shannon – such a thrill!

Some photos were then taken to mark the occasion and they returned home on their bicycles, tired but pleased, after a busy exciting day.

Fr Ryan's Legion of Mary outing to Holy Island

... and the dog came too!

As it was a 'mixed group' there was much jollity on the way back to Scariff, and with many promises to meet up again during the holidays – and maybe another boat trip!

The school outing

Students from around the country at Carrigaholt

Bicycle Power

One lovely summer evening Carmel, Nora and myself were sitting on the edge of the footpath, we were talking and making footprints on the soft tar – we were barefoot. It had been a very busy day with much playing and several chores also. Heads bent, we were unaware that anyone was beside us until we noticed that a bicycle had just stopped – Auntie Gertie. She had come all the way on her bike, pedalling the long way from Ballyvaughan. She had just spent two great weeks on holiday there and thought that she would like to give us a call before returning to Galway. Ballyvaughan was approximately forty miles away and she did not seem in the least tired.

We jumped up to welcome her and to help carry in her suitcase which was tied to the back carrier of the bike. Suddenly she was like the pied piper, surrounded by six to eight of us – nieces and neighbours. We followed her through our hall to the kitchen at the back. Mam was very surprised, but pleased to see her sister. We were shooed outside, but nobody took the slightest notice. When Auntie Gertie opened her suitcase we were glad that we had stayed. As well as her clothes, the case held biscuits, a tin of bulls' eyes, a tin of butterscotch, two bars of soft chocolate and three jars of lovely homemade, fruity, black-currant jam. Such a feast! She divided everything between us all – except the jam, which Mam quickly put out in the scullery. Then we were told to go outside again, and we were happy to have another half-hour or so with our friends. We thanked our aunt and she told us she would stay for three or four days. We were delighted to have such a pleasant visitor, so we were glad to sit outside again, some on the path edge and some on the doorstep, sucking our bulls' eyes and keeping the rest of the goodies for the following day.

Right through her life, Auntie Gertie loved to visit unexpectedly and always brought something nice with her. Once, when she was in her seventies and with a bad knee, she walked from where the bus dropped her as far as our house. This was a walk of over two miles and she was carrying a birthday gift for our daughter!

She always had a fund of stories, funny stories and 'ghostie' stories too. She was a great one for chatting late into the night – or should I say morning? However, she was a master at cat napping during the daytime, several 'naps' a day. I remember chatting to her in her kitchen one afternoon when she suddenly dozed off and had a lovely dream. I sat where I was and after a while she blinked awake, sat still for a few moments before she remembered that I was sitting near her in the room. Then she looked at me, smiled whimsically and said 'isn't it funny, for a minute there when I woke up and heard the clock ticking I thought I was back again in Ballyvaughan – isn't that strange, Colette?'

Then she quickly closed her eyes again and soon she was deeply asleep, trying to catch up on the earlier dream, I suppose. I sat there with her in the quiet afternoon doing my knitting. Occasionally a smile hovered and she chuckled softly in her sleep. Though outwardly old and frail, I'd say that in her dreams lived a woman forever young.

Mam [left] and Gertie on their bicycles

Lovely Lahinch

I suppose because we spent so much time beside the sea at Ballyvaughan, Belharbour and Galway, we didn't visit Lahinch until the early 1960s. Since then, of course, it has become one of our favourite places. It would be bliss indeed if it weren't so crowded in summertime and if car parking spaces were easier to find. Still, it has such a lovely beach, great walks around the sand dunes for our dog and ourselves and because we are very likely to meet many of our friends walking the prom it has great charm for the family and we feel comfortable and at home there.

During the war years there was an army base at Lahinch – or a military camp as it was called. You can only imagine the excitement generated in the area at the thought of a few hundred or so young men in uniform – on their own! Naturally then, the social activity of the area was built around the military base and eventually Sunday night dancing began there.

During June, July and August the famous West Clare Railway narrow line train came from Ennis every day – full to capacity. Indeed, isn't the very thought

Taking the air at Lahinch in 1947

of the 'West Clare' romantic in itself? However, the excursion train on Sundays brought crowds flocking to the seaside and with it a hundred or so girls ready for dancing and maybe a little romance.

The dances continued during the wintertime too and as time went on, it became the place to hold the dress dances such as the farmers', creamery managers' and guards' dress dances.

When the 'West Clare' finally hung up her shovels, as it were, CIE ran a diesel train from Ennis to Lahinch and a child in a pram was allowed to travel free of charge. Apparently, some of the 'children in prams' were four and five years of age!

You can believe that visiting Lahinch has memories and tradition for people around the country, but especially people in Clare, and Ennis in particular.

Lahinch is still one of the friendliest, most welcoming, of seaside spots and a great place for a bit of golf too.

Making hay in the Burren – [front] Ena and Maura
[back] Mr Cunneen, Bríd, Pádraig and unknown boy who was the best worker!

Fanore and the 'Rockies'

Our Dad liked Lahinch and visited it a few times while he was attached to the garda barracks at Fanore, but for him, nothing could compare with Fanore, Ballyvaughan and Belharbour. He was stationed at Fanore from October 1928 to December 1934 and enjoyed his time there. He always lovingly referred to it as the 'Rockies' and I suppose that if you come from the lush farmlands of north Cork it is a very appropriate name indeed. The guards lived in the barracks and next door, Sergeant O'Meara and his wife – a genial couple.

On the look out in the Burren!

There were no patrol cars or garda cars at their disposal then, so they cycled everywhere and as Fanore came under the Lisdoonvarna division they frequently attended there too. Some of the duties included checking for lights on bikes, taking care to be aware of the drunk and disorderly, and making sure that the cases I've mentioned and petty theft were dealt with

Guards from the Lisdoonvarna Division

in court. They made friends with the community and were on call if an accident or a fracas happened in the area. During his time in Fanore, Dad spent a happy few months in Carron on relief duty.

Dad met Mam shortly after he came to Fanore while she was on holiday with her uncle, Paddy O'Donoghue, in the village. I don't think it was love at first sight, but it certainly did not take them too long to find that they had a lot in common – including love. We still have some of their letters and cards exchanged over the following few years and they are very romantic indeed.

In Scariff from December 1934 he enjoyed patrol duties on the streets. Street duty was a must in those days and I am convinced that if we still had a more visible garda presence, there would be less crime in our villages and towns.

In a town like Scariff, the 'fair days' and some of the fights that went with them then were a worry for us children – until Dad came home safely.

In the summer, he covered the Bodyke area taking information for what he called Agricultural Statistics. He often brought me, on Mam's bike, out the country with him when I had time off from school.

Dad spent twenty good years in Scariff and died there while on duty. It was only after he died that we heard from people whom he had helped to keep in touch with their families in England and America, by writing their letters and then reading the replies to them. I know he would have added little extra bits of news and special greetings in an effort to bring the families closer.

We'll be busy today!

Burren Magic

Staying with our grandaunts, Hannah and Katie, long ago, was a special time. A kind of lazy funny time and we adored them. They lived in the heart of the Burren in a cosy white-washed cottage, with a sea inlet – a sort of private pool – almost over their back garden wall. The house was removed from the road too, and in the summer it was a lovely walk from the road through a field red with dainty, swaying poppies, over the hill to the farmhouse. They were very kind, the aunts, and they enjoyed having us to stay as they always loved company.

At night, we slept in a press bed. A comfortable soft bed opened out from a press in their tiny sitting-room and it held the three of us, three gigglers as my mother would say! At that time we would and could laugh at anything – and nothing!

It amused us greatly too when breakfast was over and they would say in their kindly way 'Sit out now in the street, and get the sun and the sea air.' We usually laughed loudly at the idea of the street, not a car in sight or a sound to be heard except the hens who were always busily 'working' the yard, or should I say the street. The geese could be very noisy in their own way too and they'd chase you if you gave a screech at all or ran from them. If you ran in the front door and closed it after you, forgetting how the door was made, they would fly

Where Hannah and Katie grew up in Ballyvaughan

in over the half door after you! And then, what a commotion!

Most of the time we were in Belharbour was spent eating, swimming, reading and sunbathing. Hannah and Katie were delighted to look after us and we were happy to let them. Auntie Gertie often came over from Galway while we were there and our cousin Geraldine came to play with my youngest sister, Ena.

Patsy, our sister who lived in Galway, visited at other times of the year and our grandaunts were delighted with the company. When Katie died and Hannah was alone, Patsy spent several months there and

Ballyvaughan on a quiet day!

was a great help and very good company for Hannah who was feeling lost and alone. During the long autumn and winter months, Patsy cycled every other day into Ballyvaughan and shopped for them. She cycled to neighbours' homes too and shopped for some of the older or housebound friends. She brought back the news of the day to Hannah. She enjoyed being there and found that the time flew as she was always busy.

To us, Hannah and Katie were a special part of our childhood and our growing years. Katie, until she retired, was a dressmaker and she made warm bodices each autumn for us. They were something like the gilets that are worn nowadays – though the bodices then were buttoned, not zipped. As Hannah was a knitter we were well catered for and warm and snug too.

We now have another Hannah Kate, our youngest granddaughter and a lovely lively girl she is. She went from crawling to running, why waste time walking when you can dash? And you should see her dash. She is sure-footed and knows what she wants, she mostly wants to be out of doors – in fact she always wants to be out of doors. Even when I admire her lovely curls and tell her how pretty she is, she looks me in the eye and smiling sweetly demands 'wellies, Gramma, wellies'.

A Great 'Hay' Day

I can still, when I think about it, smell the hay. A pot-pourri of fragrant clover, daisies and sun-kissed grass – and I can remember the day, vividly!

After breakfast, Granddad announced that he was drawing the hay from the Inch field and invited us holiday-makers to ride on the hay-float with him. We had great fun on the trip from the farm on the empty float. But we had more fun sitting at the back of the hay or standing unsteadily against it – not to be recommended, mind you. These days of tidy, plastic-wrapped bales hold no magic for today's children, but long ago, making hay and weeks later bringing it home was the stuff of which pleasant memories are made.

Mind you, the ride in the hay-car was a teeth-rattling, bottom-bumping sensation. The wheels did not have tyres or tubes; they were just large iron wheels, purely functional and hard on the roads. We sang loudly as we rattled along on the outward journey and Granddad's lovely voice joined in 'Daisy, Daisy', 'Ghost Riders in the Sky' and because we were in north Cork – 'The Banks of My Own Lovely Lee'. On the return journey we tickled each other, chewed hay and clung on for dear life, sitting in the tiny space at the back edge of the float.

On the particular day, I had an early start. Jumping quickly from my bed at seven, I went with Auntie Nelly to collect the cows from the Blackwater field.

Paddy Crotty mowing the hay [1953]

Nowadays I am not too bright in the early hours, but back then I loved that special time, particularly if we were on the farm. Nelly was funny and had a great love of nature. She would point out baby rabbits skipping about and occasionally she would be thrilled to show me the ladybirds on a food safari on a nasturtium leaf.

Back in the byre I spent some time leaning against Dora – Dora was my favourite cow. Nelly ping-pinged milk into an enamel bucket and every so often squirted milk into a dish a few yards away. The dish was quickly licked clean by the farm cats. They had their own part to play in the scheme of things – helping to keep the farm rodent-free.

Breakfast that morning was the usual lightly boiled egg, brown bread and then wild strawberries and thick cream from the dairy. Such luxury! Then we were sent to our bedroom for a quick wash, using water from the ewer. The ewer was a large jug that as a rule had a matching basin. They were patterned too and looked quite pretty, though to be honest I preferred to use running water from the tap like we had in the scullery at home. Anyway I washed, a

We just have to read 'Curly Wee'!

Heading out to work!

sort of a 'lick and a promise' as Mam would say and I vowed to have a good wash before going to bed that night. I hurried into my clothes because Granddad didn't like to waste time, especially on this beautiful 'blue day'. The previous day had been very wet until the late afternoon.

My blouse was seersucker, a new fabric that happily did not have to be ironed. I had sewn my dirndl skirt myself with the help of my good neighbour and friend, Mrs Cunneen. In fact, she had given me a present of the material too, and I was very proud of it. It was green cotton with a butterfly border at the end and two large pockets where I could store some sweets and biscuits. I knew I looked nice and it made me feel good. Best of all, I had on my brand new pink underwear with the good elastic – isn't there something very comforting about new underwear? No worries that the waist elastic would hang loosely! Sitting tightly at the back end of the float, I secretly admired my best ankle socks – white with narrow green stripes – and my polished brown sandals. I loved dressing up and with my thick, coarse, red hair and skin covered with freckles I felt I needed all the help I could get to make me look well. Carefully glancing sideways at my sister, Sheelagh, I had to admit that though she was two years younger she made a very pretty eight year old. Our youngest sister, Ena, sat in front with Granddad where he could keep an eye on her. Our two older cousins, May and John, shared the narrow shelf at the back.

I settled my head against the warm hay, smoothed my skirt and sneaked a clove drop out of my pocket. Eyes closed, I sucked my sweet, blissfully un-aware of the waterlogged gap into the farm – our hay route to the barn!

Occasionally the bumping and rattling made one painfully bite a lip or the inside of a cheek, or worse still, chokingly swallow a sweet! I was having a lovely daydream, the sun was hot on my face, but for once I did not worry about getting more freckles. Suddenly it seemed as if my stomach lurched for-ward as the float went down into a deep sink, as Auntie Nelly would call it. The horse and float continued without stopping, leaving me, as it dipped at the back, sitting up to the top of my pink underwear in dirty water!

I tried to scream, but found that the shock had left me speechless. The three who had shared the ledge were still on it and seemed quite unconcerned about my plight. So, I dragged myself out and walked uncomfortably back to the house – a mucky trail behind me. I dreaded facing in the door to Nelly, as she might be very cross. One look at me and she threw herself down on the settle, gave a strangled screech and I realised that she was laughing and laughing and could not stop.

I stripped off carefully and put the muddy clothes into a galvanised bucket and then had a good wash, reminding myself that I was lucky I hadn't wasted the water earlier as it had to be drawn from a well or collected in a barrel if it rained. In a striped pinny, loose underwear and barefoot, I ventured into the kitchen again. She had almost stopped laughing, she straightened her face and said 'well Colette, look at it this way, you can join me now for milk and choco-late biscuits and next time round you'll be ready for the gap and you'll hold on.' And she was right and we had such fun. I can still smell the hay!

The pony and trap to Mass was a luxury and quite a novelty for us visitors. After Mass, there was the ice cream, the chatter, and the banter with Nelly and her friends. Then, for the men, there was porter.

Ah yes, those were the days of home-cured bacon and chipolata sausages, oil stoves and stewing tea; lively card games around the fire with much 'friendly', loud, arguing over who should have played what and funny stories and yarns too. It was the time of going barefoot in the meadow with tea from large bottles. We had tiny wood splinters in our bare thighs from the hay-float, and hay-seed in our knickers from playing around the hay-shed. There were treasures in the hay-loft, mice and frogs and outside smelly pigs in their sty.

Best of all, sleeping on a snug, feathered tick, between lavender-scented sheets in a mellow cosy room – a room full of memories.

Our Games

During the summer we played many ball games as well as board games. I played tennis, hurling and badminton, but I really wasn't very good. I did enjoy being part of the fun involved, but really I was never what you would call 'pretty good' at any sport. There were many things that I felt happy and good at and indeed it was difficult at times to fit everything in to any spare time so I was not disappointed. We always went to hurling matches though, especially when we were older and could admire the 'talent'.

Dad played hurling and football, but he loved football especially. He played with the local team while he lived at home in Cork, but it was not very easy to travel for training in those days once he joined the guards. But he did play with them when he was at home on holidays. Mam was very good at camogie and she and her sisters were very active members of Galway's Westonians Camogie Club. However, once she was married she did not continue to play with her club – distance again being the problem. She always kept up the game and even when she was grandmother to young teenagers, she hurled with them and enjoyed the exercise. Without any difficulty she could hit a ball from one end of the field to the other. Ena played camogie when she was young too, and she was good.

Anyone for tennis?

I've often said how much I enjoy playing board games, card games or running about with our grandchildren. But it was with great joy, that by accident, I discovered a few years ago that I was quite good at football! I was sixty at the time and you can imagine the thrill it gave me. I can still hold my own playing with our grandchildren and kicking hard with my left foot!

Men in Suits

Long ago we made sure that we 'brushed up well' and we would not be seen at an outing unless our dirndl skirts were well washed and starched and we had socks matching our outfits in the summertime. In the winter, we wore flared wool skirts mostly stitched by ourselves, carefully ironed and with handknitted sweaters to complement the skirts.

The men, we felt, had it much easier because the one good suit could take them right through the year if they were careful. A crisp white shirt and stiff collar might be needed on formal occasions, but apart from that the suit took them everywhere.

All dressed up – and nowhere to go!

Perhaps because our Dad mostly wore a uniform, we rarely saw him in a suit except on holidays or on family occasions. In those days gardaí were encouraged to wear their uniforms as much as possible. While this was cosy and warm, worn under the great coat in the winter, the heavy scratchy wool of the jacket with its high mandarin collar made the outfit most uncomfortable in the summertime. However, the care Dad took with his uniform was a lesson for us. He always felt that we owe it to ourselves, and to those we meet, to have shoes shined, hair neat, clothes dusted and brushed and in the case of a suit – a razor sharp crease on the trousers!

Men in suits – lovely!

So, I suppose I grew up admiring men in suits and men in well-cared-for suits particularly. I do remember how nice it was to see the men in suits, young men especially, standing in groups and chatting. I think it made the younger ones particularly feel grown up when they stood with feet apart, hands in their pockets and a wisp of straw maybe between the teeth. It pleases me to think about it, indeed it still gives me a thrill.

Teachers and trainees at Scoil Bhrighde

Gaeltacht Holidays

Seán spent two very enjoyable years in Cork city in the middle of the 1950s while attending Scoil Bhrighde. His bicycle was very much part of him and he cycled from his digs in Sunday's Well to the school, and he got to know the city very well. Pedalling along the Mardyke, Grand Parade, 'Pana' and the Western Road gave a great sense of freedom. You can just imagine how much he and his classmates enjoyed the independence of their own transport. Seán and I were not dating at the time, but I was on holiday with Auntie Chrissie in north Cork when I saw a photo of Seán and his friends in the *Cork Examiner*. I kept the photo for years.

During their time at Scoil Bhrighde they travelled by bus the long distance from Cork to the Gaeltacht at Loughanure in Donegal, where they were to spend the summer months. Naturally, the bikes were carefully tied to the top of the bus – they would need them to get around the Gaeltacht area. Even though the weather was warm, they not only brought their bicycles, but they were in their good suits too. So, when their bus got stuck under the railway bridge at Gort, because of the bicycles on top, everyone had to get to work. The bikes had to come down and then the bus drove through – easily. Next, the bikes had to be carefully put back on top of the bus and secured – and the suits did not get a speck on them!

The good news – they had a brilliant time in Loughanure. Seán always said that the time he spent there was very happy and that he would love to go back for a visit.

He did – we went back there together.

High notions!

Musical Delights

Dad had a lovely way of walking with the blackthorn. He held it, let us say, loosely in his hand and swung it in front of him with each lively step. In the winter evenings, especially when it was wet and cold, he would place his good blackthorn on the kitchen floor and cross it with a lighter one – his second best stick I suppose. He would get us to dance – the dance that he had already shown us – while he sang the music for us. 'I went in to a tailor's shop, and I picked up a needle, the tailor came out and gave me a shout – pop goes the weasel' – they were more or less the words for a nice tuneful bit of music. It was a very bouncy, warming, whooping kind of a dance – if you know what I mean. I haven't danced it for ages, but I think I will try it. I will teach it to our grand-children when next they come to see us. Talking of blackthorn, the hedges at the back of our home are alive with blackthorn in flower at the moment. When the early sun lights the blackthorn, it lights the heart too.

Our neighbours, the Cunneens, owned a gramophone. They had a piano and a harmonium too. But Nora and myself loved the gramophone best of all and the records we played on it were classical. They were the only records in the house and Mozart was our favourite. Of course all of this was before we had radio or electricity and the gramophone had to be 'wound up' – but this did not bother us in the least.

Mozart was our favourite then and still is to this day. The records which we almost wore out were 'Eine Kleine' as we called it, and the 'Andante, piano concerto 21 in C' – Elvira Madigan.

Mozart can still give me a warm glow and maybe a teeny heartache for those lovely early years.

Mozart is best!

Doting Grandparents

Whenever we talked of growing up and marrying, and we never thought that we would not marry, we often chatted about how many children we might like to have. We all had quite definite ideas, but the thoughts of grandchildren never entered our consciousness at all, nor did the idea that we might be fortunate to be around long enough to grow old.

Having enjoyed our own children, we are now in our sixties and enjoying our grandchildren. We find them engaging, amusing, enchanting, refreshing, loveable – and tiring! We enjoy spending time with them and then it is nice to hand them back to their parents so that 'Grampa' and I can relax and get our wind back.

I love to dance, to dance in a ballroom or even around the house if the mood takes me. Our grandchildren often join us in 'Shoe the donkey' or the graceful 'Charleston' – up and down the kitchen to our own humming, a tape or CD. Auntie Gertie taught my sisters and me to dance the Charleston many years ago – when we were young and beautiful! She was particularly good at the Charleston and was an excellent teacher. Because she loved to dance she never tired of dancing with us, or showing us new steps. Somehow, over the busy, busy years we did not dance the Charleston at all, I do not know why, and we forgot the steps. Then, last autumn, we learnt it again. I cannot begin to tell you how much I love to dance it. It has a certain grandeur and dignity to it and the movements are elegant and fast. The dance too has a lovely charming air about it, in short – it's terrific! I could dance the Charleston all day and our grandchildren love it too.

Like most people nowadays, we are 'hands-on' grandparents and will happily involve ourselves in any game and often invent games. In truth, our own grandparents were pretty special and gave us their time too. I must say that when James, Ben, Alannah, Hannah and Eoin are playing with us, ours is a very noisy household indeed. After a hectic 'train game' one warm evening, I scribbled the following short piece for all of them, and called it 'just a second':

Just a second, my darling young friend, just a second, there is time we can spend. We can play, we can talk, we can garden or walk – and, dear grandchild, there's time for pretend. We can fly on a plane made from chairs and quick travel by train on the stairs, but the best fun of all when we come to the hall – and our driver calls out 'any fares'. There is magic abroad in the air, there are stories and rhymes too to share, the wind whispers softly as she goes quickly by 'I'm off to a storm – so beware!'

You are all of the dreams of my youth, and such fun we are having in truth. Time goes so quickly by in the blink of an eye, so we are weaving our memories to boot!

Having a ball at the Astor in the 1950s

Just Joking

In our teens, and to be honest. I don't know who started it, there were games we played and even though they may seem silly now, nevertheless they gave us days and evenings of quite harmless fun – and much enjoyment. One of the games was not as easy to play then as it might seem now with today's glut of cars. We had to tot up the registration number on a car until we found a car which correctly totted up to twenty-one. As cars were so scarce, this game often spread over several months – and helped us with our mental arithmetic. You see, we had to collect twenty-one twenty-ones, and twenty-five twenty-fives, if you know what I mean. Then, when the required number were finally counted – the first eligible man we met was the man we would eventually marry!

Also, if somebody was so good as to give us a finger of wedding cake, we could not eat it then no matter how tempted. The cake had to be slept on first, under the pillow, and you hoped you would dream of your future spouse!

But there was one game we enjoyed most of all and which 'happened' in the summer evenings. Us girls, three or four of us anyway, would 'doll our-selves up' and walk in a leisurely way as far as the local vocational school. The school was about, say, a mile from our homes. We did this walk for nine even-ings, and not necessarily nine consecutive evenings, you know. If the weather was rainy, we gave it a miss. Well, in truth, we loved the walk, meeting with others and maybe a chat with the lads too. Anyway, on the ninth evening, we would carefully take a leaf each from one of the flowering cherry trees. The leaf was then brought home on the palm of the hand, placed under the pillow, and slept on for a week. And surely, during that time we 'must' see our husbands-to-be in our dreams!

These games were great to get us out of doors and into the fresh air. If we did meet someone special, or dream of someone we fancied, I for one cannot remember. But I can remember the fun! I often wondered if the boys ever played such innocent games, but of course if they did they wouldn't admit it – to us anyway. I remember once, shortly before our wedding, telling Seán about our simple games and I asked if he and the lads had ever done anything like that. With a bemused look, and the quirk of an eyebrow he said, 'Ah now love, ah come on – you just have to be joking!'

Sounds I Love

There are sounds that I love, like a baby gurgling or a cat purring, rain softly falling on old thatch; a bellows stirring up a lazy fire; the comfortable drone of evening voices with everyone home and accounted for – ready for sleep. Then there are the kitchen morning sounds like the filling of the kettle; the sound of a teapot being scraped and settled on a hot coal; chairs dragged around the breakfast table, and the clatter of delft on the scrubbed old pine.

I love too the sound of different music notes. On my own, I can often try out notes that please me, and I listen to them for myself. This is, I suppose, because of the years of early training in tonic solfa, both at national school and in our youth choir. We were always happy to try out notes, and we ran up and down the scales, at will – often for the entertainment of our friends.

Do you know what I discovered recently? There are some people who aren't even singers as such, and indeed sing flat most of the time, but occasionally they make a lovely clear pure note. Then it seems as if it takes them by surprise, so they savour the note, roll it on the tongue and enjoy it for as long as possible.

Of course, in those lovely, long ago days we lived in our heads as it were. We sang constantly, hummed aloud, sang the top songs of the day and 'lilted' any classical pieces that we knew – and they were many. Before we had radio or even electricity, we made our own entertainment and if we loved a song we treasured and sang it at every opportunity, whether on our own – or with others. I often sat through a sermon at Mass and sang several songs in my head, oblivious to everyone around me. Just passing the time for myself in a favourite pleasant way. Sermons then were long, mostly fire and brimstone to varying degrees and usually boringly repetitive. So, if I passed the time 'singing in my head' I could be almost certain that my friends were likely doing the same thing; their happy expressions usually gave them away. This did not mean that we were not prayerful – for indeed we were. But sermons to us, with clear consciences, were unnecessary and something that had to be 'dismissed' as it were, by going over our repertoire of songs.

You know the way you can associate a particular food or place with a pleasant happening or a memorable occasion; well music and song can even more vividly 'call up' unforgotten happy times for me. I can relive music and pictures. I only have to hear 'Máire My Girl' and it brings to mind blissfully warm Saturday mornings in my friend Nora's garden where we sat reading *Sunny Stories* or any other Enid Blyton books we could get our hands on. Because her father had no work on this day either, he busied himself in his flower garden and sang all the old Irish airs.

Isn't it amazing the amount of stuff one can store within one's memory, and how little it can take to trigger a pen picture? I love nothing better than an afternoon or evening of reminiscing, poetry, thinking of my friends and playing music. Dad always sang 'Danny Boy' for Mam, it pleased her greatly and hearing it at any time can bring such memories. Dad died in 1954 and Mam joined him in 1998. Such a long time on her own, and such a long time without his company. She was very ill for about a year before she died in my sister Ena's home where she had happily lived for several years. Occasionally during Mam's last year we would attempt to 'doll her up' in dainty nighties and so on, but she was not having any of that. Though very frail, she was quite well able to say an emphatic 'no' to any suggestions of 'maybe you'd like this or that, Mam'.

One Sunday afternoon when Ena, Sheelagh and I were sitting with her, about two weeks before she died, she was sleeping peacefully. I sat there thinking of how proud she was of the Foxford rug she had bought when we were young and how she always treasured it. Looking at her sleeping, I thought how right she was not to surround herself with unfamiliar things now that her days were spent mostly drifting in and out of sleep. As we sat there, I wrote these few lines for her. At the time I called it 'Wishes for you' and it was written with love and thanks:

> You should now have the very softest cushions, in shades of faded pinks and lightest blue; to soften the tired paleness and the shadows that line your face – still beautiful 'tis true.
>
> You should have sheets of finest silk placed lightly, and touching them feel special and much more; but you want your old pillows that hold memories and your warm splendid rug you bought of yore.
>
> But when you close your eyes and take to dreaming, we can tell by how serenely you lie there that in your dreams you are not ill and dying and your body is not tired and worn so spare.
>
> In dreams you skip so lightly in the Burren, held by the hand whose touch you've missed for long: And shortly you will visit special places, and join him as he sings you a lovely old sweet song.

Other songs that come to mind, with childhood memories, are the hauntingly beautiful 'I Hear You Calling Me' and the lively 'Kerry Dances'. Those songs remind me of evenings standing outside Granddad's home in Gortmore, listening to the pure, clear, tenor voice as he sang for himself, sitting in front of the fire and unaware of an audience. He sang for many an audience in his younger days, on his own and with his brothers. He sang in the choir too and he sang as he drove the pony and trap to Mass, and sang for any occasion for his family and friends. He could be heard daily too, when he walked the cows down home to be milked.

But when he was old, he mostly sang for himself. By the time we got to know him, he was in his late sixties or in his early seventies. By then the voice, apparently, had lost some of its early energy, but we thought he was great anyway – and indeed he was. In his late seventies he lost his sight and as if by compensation for the loss, his voice took on again some of the clearness of earlier years and had a happy lilt to it too.

Music for the soul, the heart and the mind!

Granddad always sang in the meadow after a cuppa

Fair Days

How things change. I was just thinking the other day how my younger sister and her friends loved to visit a corpse house, as they called it. They went there, not just to pray for the dead – but to get lemonade and biscuits. They often spent entire afternoons and part of the evening in the home of the person who had died. It was very much the custom then, though not so much now, to keep the body in the house overnight – to pray for the dead and to give them one last night at home. Of course, there had to be something to eat and drink, especially for the people who stayed during the night to keep the bereaved company. Sheelagh and her friends never missed a funeral until Mam became aware of their visits and put a stop to it – until they were older anyway.

On the evening of the removal of the person to the church, the shops always closed their doors and those in private houses pulled down their window blinds until the cortege had passed and similarly next day on the way to the graveyard. We often peeped from behind the blind at the crowd passing by, when we were considered too young to attend. We were warned not to count the cars, few as they might be at the time. I imagine that this was because of some superstition or other. Mind you I would feel a little uneasy even now, if I became aware that somebody was counting vehicles at a funeral.

I was thinking too, among other things, of the fair day. That same fair day was a great nuisance for those of us living in the town who did not have anything to gain from it. It meant cow dung at the front door, cows looking in the windows and investigating the doorway whenever one tried to open a door. It meant the lowing of the cattle at an unearthly hour outside one's home, and the loud chat and shouts of the drovers and buyers.

Now if it happened to be a wet day, and indeed I remember many wet fair days, it meant cow dung in the hallway and all over the house. But, the fair day also meant a day away from school, a day once a month in which we did not have to study! On fair days too, when overmuch alcohol was imbibed, rows often erupted and then the gardaí would be called to intervene in the rows and fights. Because we lived opposite the fair green, our Dad often had to answer one of these calls, and this always upset me greatly. You see, when people are engaged in fisticuffs, they don't mind who they hit. Dad sometimes came off worse than those he had gone to help.

Still, in the summertime, I mostly liked the fair – especially as I grew older and had an eye for a handsome farmer!

Bishops' Quarter Graveyard – overlooking Black Head and the sea

Fair day in the 1930s

Beloved Dolls

We had the best-dressed dolls – without question. Whatever the season or occasion, our dolls wore the very latest fashions and had their outfits changed a few times daily too. There was very little money around, for extras, in the 1940s. Most of us, in truth, just owned a Sunday best and perhaps a few hand-me-downs for weekdays, but we were fortunate for several reasons that we lived next door to Kathleen and Nora. Nora loved to cook and to bake and had infinite patience with us children. Kathleen was an excellent seamstress and she was constantly busy with winter coats, spring suits and summer dresses. She also made outfits for weddings and special occasions. I loved to stand at her high work-table, just looking at her tacking a garment or carefully removing the tacking from a finished outfit. The knotted 'tack thread' was then tidily placed in a small tin box for re-use.

The sisters were quiet unassuming people who always answered our many questions and who listened to our little problems and shared our joys; they were very special to us indeed. On dark, dreary wet days, or really just because we felt like sewing, we would ask 'Kathleen, can we go through your pieces bag please?' This question, in fact, was a mere formality because Kathleen always nodded 'Yes'. The excitement! We could go through the bag and have a good root, or better still, we were frequently allowed to empty the contents onto the kitchen floor. From this hoard, we would choose material for a new dress or coat, suit or hat for the dolls.

Some materials were stiff and tweedy, but there were satins and silk too – and cotton. The fashion shades of that year ended up on our dolls. I well remember when seersucker and waffle first arrived and we made tiny summer dresses with hats to match. The dolls had several dirndl skirts too because, you see, dirndls were very much in fashion around that time.

We either sewed in our own homes, or each side of Nora's warm turf fire and listened to their battery radio. It was sheer luxury just sitting there in comfort, sewing and absorbing the music and chat. I remember many, many happy afternoons and evenings with my sisters and our best friends, designing, cutting out, sewing and fitting on. Fitting on, you see, was most important. We were aware of this because Kathleen fitted outfits on us which were not for us at least once a day. We had to stand quite still while we were pinned, chalked, snipped and tacked; and though we never ever said so to Kathleen, we didn't always willingly fit on the clothes. If we were busy sewing, or indeed if we were very busy outside playing, one of us was always bound to be called in to fit on the clothes for owners who weren't within 'hailing' distance.

So, you can be quite sure that our dolls had very many 'fit-ons' during the making. We had learned much from watching Kathleen, so the doll's clothes were carefully made and nicely finished. One of the things I really loved was cutting out with the big scissors. Now it wasn't just the cutting or the scissors that I loved, and still do, but it was the heavy sound of the scissors as it slipped along the table, cutting through the material, in the centre of the chalk line.

We took great comfort from the fact that even if, at times, we resembled 'raggedy Ann', the dolls were always dressed up and ready to grace any occasion.

Well, as they say, those were the days, such simple pleasures, such happy times.

Waiting for the bus with our Nancy doll

Our favourite dolls

Our dolls came everywhere!

Summer Holidays

We were fortunate that Dad was a Corkman and that Mam was from Galway. We had two places at least for a proper holiday each year. This was great for the parents too as we could be 'left' in each house, with doting relatives, for a few weeks at a time.

Granny, in Galway, had been widowed when Mam was about six years old. With six other children to care for, including baby Frank who was only about three at the time, I am sure she was happy and relieved when her mother in Ballyvaughan, took Mam and Auntie Gertie to stay for a few years. They continued with their schooling and loved the life there, and after school their grandmother taught them to make rag rugs. At least an hour each afternoon was spent working on the rugs and because their Aunt Katie was a dressmaker there was no shortage of spare material which was cut into strips to suit, then the girls were shown how to hook the strips into sacking. A pattern of colour was nicely worked into the rugs and the style of the finished rug depended on the pieces available. When Mam and Aunt Gertie did return to Galway, they came back to Ballyvaughan, Fanore and Belharbour at every opportunity.

Granny, however, had to settle in Galway with the rest of the family. I think that she liked being there. She loved to cook and she loved to garden too, though I do not know where she got the time to spare – or indeed the money either. I am told that I resemble her and certainly I inherited her red hair and freckles. Strangely enough, my paternal grandfather had the same auburn hair also and yet my parents were both black-haired and my siblings were dark-haired as well. Grandfather was widowed when we knew him, but we considered ourselves fortunate indeed that we had a Granny and a Granddad though at opposite ends of the country – and neither too far distant from Scariff where we lived. We always had a great time in each place and I have very few memories of bad weather or wet days during our summer holidays

We adored being on the farm, but we loved the city too, each had its own charm for us. Though Granddad had a farm and a lovely flower garden, maintained by Nelly, he had a small enough vegetable plot. But, Granny in the city had a flower garden, many vegetables, and apple trees, blackcurrants, red and white currents – and hens!

Eyre Square, Galway

Through the small cottage windows, set in thick white walls, the heady smell of phlox filled my childhood bedroom when I stayed at Granddad's home each summer. And walking between the rows of those tall, sweet-smelling flowers, I found I was 'nose-level' with them for a few years. Phlox was the mainstay of that front garden patch, with just a few nasturtiums to the side. And, actually, though I loved the pretty peonies growing between the tasty black and red berries in Granny's back garden, the phlox scent stayed with me until I married and made a garden of my own.

Now, in the autumn of my life, I enjoy 'all' my garden and I feel content and fulfilled. What a blessed thing is a garden, full of memories; evocative of times past and a promise that spring always comes.

Toft's carnival was always in Eyre Square in Galway while we were on holidays and we went there nightly. The bumpers, the big wheel, swing boats and the crowd – it was sheer magic. Even if we hadn't money with us, we could still enjoy just being out and about among friends for fun and a chat, and in our teens – to eye the boys!

Granny had a small pension and yet she always gave us some money nightly for at least one of the carnival rides. Uncle Christy, who lived at home with Granny, spent a nice little sum of money on us too while we were on holiday with them. He was great company and very funny and we could 'wind him around our little fingers' or we thought we could – which is almost the same thing.

While in Galway, we walked every day to Salthill or Grattan Road with Auntie Gertie and spent several hours on the beach, swimming, paddling, playing in the sand and eating sandy banana sandwiches – and sunning ourselves!

Sometimes our neighbours from Scariff holidayed in the Grattan Road area. When we joined them for several glorious hours each day, we neglected Salthill, as it were. The Cunneens always rented a house overlooking the sea, so they were in our favourite Grattan beach spot from early breakfast each morning until their bedtime which was usually late during their holidays. We arrived at the beach after lunch and though we spent a long, long afternoon in their company, our friends were still happily playing when we left.

Our beloved Granny had a meal cooked for us when we returned to her home. After we had eaten and chatted, she would finally sit down for the evening with gentle dreamy Auntie Mary who helped her in every way. Granny loved to read and so did Mary. They read everything, magazines, books, the papers or whatever was to hand. Then, we all had a tasty filling apple cake before we went to bed.

Though our Cork holiday was quite different from our Galway time, we loved both places and adored those special people who gave holiday time and much love to a bunch of young girls, it made a great start in life for us. I often, still, think of those who gave of themselves and taught us to laugh at ourselves and have fun, not forgetting Auntie Chrissie in Cork – the funniest of all!

Goodbye in Gortmore

One lovely balmy September evening in 1953 when I returned home with the Cunneens after a few games of tennis, I heard that our Granddad in Cork had died unexpectedly. Well, he was in his eighties and not too well that summer, but we had no idea that he would leave us so soon. It was decided then that I would accompany Dad to Gortmore, near Banteer, next morning. Mam then offered, I remember, to buy some cornflakes for my breakfast instead of porridge, if I thought they would agree with me and be better for the 'bus journey'. I cannot remember now which cereal I had for breakfast, but I do know that I was slightly queasy on the bus and glad to arrive at last at Gortmore.

Dad became quite upset when we arrived – and I knew he would. Indeed, I was feeling very sad myself. There were groups of people standing around in front of the house, chatting, some smoking and all waiting to escort Mike to Banteer church. He was one of the founder members of the famous Banteer sports and was well known. Dad, the only son, was welcomed and sympathised with and I had my hand shaken too.

The house was overflowing with people and it felt very strange. I was in no hurry to enter the bedroom where Granddad lay on his own bed, but Auntie Nelly gave me a big hug and linked me into the room. I knew where the bed was, of course, and how he would lie – so I decided to look well above the bed as we walked towards it. I knelt and she did too. I felt frightened and sad; lonely for my grandfather and cross at myself as well, because I had not looked at him.

This was the man, I reminded myself, who sat me on his knee when I was small and who sang to me and told me stories; the man who loved to see us when we came each summer – and who was always sad to see us go. He let me fish with him too in the Blackwater in my early years. Many years later he loved to sit on an ivy-covered stone seat in the hedge across the road from his house and regale us with stories and songs. And on wet days we would sit on the settle under the wide chimney piece while he sat opposite on his armchair and automatically swung the bellows. He was a great talker and we enjoyed the many stories and songs on those wet hours and he encouraged us to try out our songs too.

And yet, I had not looked at him. I was afraid, I suppose, that he would appear very, very changed. I gave an involuntary deep sigh and Nelly put an encouraging arm around my shoulders. There was a great sound of chat and prayers, coming in to the room, from the rest of the house and from outside it.

Dad and some of the others had joined us in the room by now, so I moved my gaze a little. The first thing I noticed on top of the wardrobe was Grand-dad's lovely hat – slightly dusty as if it had not been in use for awhile. Though we had visited Gortmore in early July, I could not remember if the hat was being worn then, but I felt sure that he had been wearing it. Next to the hat, was an old shoe-box which I knew was full of his own special things, like fishing flies – and hand-tied ones at that! I knew there were old photographs in the box too, and cartridges for the shotgun. I did not like the gun and always felt sorry for the rabbits, but of course, grandfather had not used the gun for several years. However, long ago, if you were with him on a rabbit hunt, and if you made a sound at all, he would wither you with a look and you didn't feel too popular at all.

Just then, I heard a cricket. We always heard crickets in Gortmore and not anywhere else, I wonder why? I listened for the crickets again and heard them and I was aware too of the occasional burst of laughter from outside and it bothered me, though nobody else took any notice at all. Glancing towards the wash-stand, I saw his fishing rod standing neatly behind it and this was almost my undoing. But it finally gave me the courage to look, and he was just the same, how could I have thought otherwise? His remaining faded, grey-red hair was carefully combed, and his bushy eyebrows were as wiry as ever. As we stood up, Nelly said 'how happy and peaceful he looks'.

And yes he did, and I was glad I had seen this for myself, very glad.

Granddad

Back Yard Treasures

Our back yard was very small and we didn't have a garden attached to it either, but as our Dad was the only guard interested in sowing vegetables in the barrack garden, we looked on it as our own. In that garden, he grew carrots, parsnips, onions, vegetable marrow and some potatoes. We children enjoyed the garden and we helped occasionally, though not always successfully, but we loved the produce. Dad also sowed potatoes out the country where he had 'a few drills' as he said himself. So, we were very well looked after in that area and actually never felt the loss of a back garden.

Though the yard was small, there was a shed in it, open at the front and with a galvanised roof. At one side was a tiny enclosed run for the hens, and at the other, the party wall between our yard and Kathleen and Nora's – and their shed too. Their shed was very much tidier than ours, but definitely not as interesting. In ours was a perch at the back that Dad had made for the hens. Underneath the perch were three or four old enamel or tin basins that had seen better days. These basins were made quite comfortable for our hens with nice twists of hay from Son Rodgers' hay-shed nearby.

With all that comfort, our hens produced some tasty brown eggs every day. The hens were Rhode Island Reds and we were quite fond of them. In the shed too, was the turf that Dad had brought home from the bog, it lasted the entire year. The turf was neatly stacked, though I can tell you that when it was delivered to our back gate it was a backbreaking job to spend an afternoon and evening carrying it into the shed and stacking it. All hands helped then and we had some willing neighbours too. Afterwards, in the kitchen, we had layers of dropscones and if Mam hadn't had to spend too much time carrying in the turf, we would have a few apple tarts and maybe hot gingerbread as well.

I always found that for days afterwards we could still comb out turf dust and blow it from the nose. And we could taste it too, all evening and maybe even into the next day! But the unpleasant bits aside, we felt happy and secure when our turf was safely in.

We had four ducks too and their laying boxes were in the shed as well. Regularly, well at least once a week in the summertime, and every other week for the rest of the year, Dad would block the drain in the yard and turn on the

Waiting for the ducks in the back yard

tap in the scullery. He would allow the water to rise and come out around the yard a bit, though never near the shed. The excitement of the ducks was a joy to see and how noisy and happy they always were in the water! Do you know, whenever I hear someone say 'it's a great day for ducks' it always brings me back, and I can see them splashing and washing and shuffling and generally having a good time. This 'noise' would go on for an hour or two until they finally came out of the water themselves, to a dry part of the yard, or into the shed. Then the water was allowed down the drain, for that day. Our yard always looked nice and clean when it dried afterwards.

Mam always made a fuss of a clocking hen and I remember, once, seeing her pull a hen from its hay basin as an egg was about to open – the only egg in there. We all stared in shock and there was this tiny, fluffy chick on its own – Bunty had arrived. Mam had not realised that the hen was hatching, or if she did she must have overlooked it. The excitement! You can imagine it. Whenever we had a 'clocking hen' Mam would dispatch one of us to Flannerys, across the road for a setting of eggs. I could not understand for years why we did not use our own hen eggs!

But the funniest thing, and we still laugh over it from time to time, was when four or five of us friends joined the hens in the shed if it was warm, but raining. On a day such as this, we would not want to be indoors and yet we needed a shelter over our heads. Dad had fixed a swing in the shed with a strong rope from the front beam and it had a comfortable wooden seat too. We took turns on the swing and loved it. Of course, you couldn't swing very high at all or you could damage your head off the inside of the shed. So, on a damp though mild day, one of us would take the swing and sit and swing and chat for maybe ten minutes and then it was the turn of someone else, and so on. Those not on the swing, usually four, sat on basins of hay; lovely fresh hay from Son's hay-shed and the basins from our cubbies – and we pretended to 'hatch'!

Of course, in a way, I suppose you could say we were hatching, as we chatted and rested and generally had a lovely, lazy, friendly afternoon together. We were full of ideas and ready for a giggle, and if you have never spent an afternoon on soft hay, hatching, you just do not know what you have been missing!

In the summer, we often spent long afternoons and early evenings catching minnows, in a jam jar. I do not really know why we did this, but possibly because we enjoyed messing about in a few inches of water – and actually catching something. We usually had a jam jar each and we were very careful to ensure that they would not get cracked or broken. If we were unlucky enough to break a jar in the water, we had to collect all the glass in case anyone inadvertently walked on it and got cut. It is difficult enough to see glass at the bottom of a sandy and stony stream. But the main reason, I think, why we were so careful with the jars is that in those days we could sell a jam jar in good condition to any of the local shops and earn a few welcome pennies.

Apart from the enjoyment of messing about in the water, I can never understand now, why we bothered to bring the minnows home. You could be quite sure that if they weren't dead by the time we brought them home, they would certainly be found floating on top of the water soon afterwards.

To mess about in the water we had to put up our skirts or dresses carefully into our knickers' leg elastic. If we did not do this, our clothes might get wet, indeed they would get wet without a doubt. But by putting them into the elastic, we were stretching the elastic and this wasn't a good idea at all. From being rolled up in tight elastic, the skirts when loosened came down wrinkled a few hours later. If you were very unlucky, they were still wrinkled the next day!

There is so much comfort with children's clothes nowadays and they are so practical. But, do the children still go catching a minnow? That, as they say, is the question!

The stream we visited so often was on the way to the church and we called it the Lane River. We mostly did our fishing under the bridge and it was often quite crowded in there! I am not really into fishing now and for that matter, I have lost interest in trying to trap a minnow in a jam jar, or in my hand. But if I had to fish with a grandchild, I would. But I would prefer to sit on the bank and watch, or to the side and supervise. I must be getting old!

In the fishing season, Dad fished almost every day, even if only for a short while. Whenever he fished, we had lovely trout for the tea. He always brought back the fish gutted, cleaned and ready for the pan. Wasn't it a luxury to eat fish as fresh as they were? Sometimes, though, he threw back small trout and I imagine that if he did not like the flavour as much as he did, he would return all the catch to the water. This, because he was an angler at heart and it was the thrill of the catch he enjoyed.

He fished first in the Blackwater near Banteer, from the age of five. He was 'hooked', if you like, and from then on he fished wherever he was – if he thought there were fish there. When he fished in the river Graney at Scariff, he often had an audience, especially if the trout was big and he had to 'play it'. I think Dad enjoyed his audience, he was a bit of a showman anyway, in the nicest possible

way. And, after all, weren't they all locals and friends?

I remember, once when Carmel, Nora and I were returning from a walk, we saw people leaning over a bridge below the town. We did not have any fear that somebody had fallen in, but we joined the group and watched Dad as he expertly, and with ease, played a big trout and eventually caught him – or 'landed' him.

I was very proud of him that evening, but to be honest, I was always proud of our Dad anyway and I loved him dearly.

Dad – with his favourite rod

Swimming and Sailing

My husband Seán learned to swim at the O'Curry Irish College in Carrigaholt, and from the influence of the principal Buadhac Tóibín, who owned a lovely motor boat, he developed a fascination with boats, the water and water sports, especially sailing.

For my own part, even though I enjoyed swimming when I was young and I can row a boat, I have a great fear of sailing and much prefer *terra firma*. Once, during my teens, I went out in a large sailing boat during the blessing of the bay in Galway. The boat was overcrowded and the skipper had taken more alcohol than he could cope with, but worst of all, conditions at sea were very rough. We were all very relieved to come safely ashore and realised that we were lucky to be alive. Though this happened about fifty years ago, I can still, when I think of it, feel the absolute terror and fear during the short time at sea, and the relief when we stood ashore.

For Seán, the scarier the conditions in the water, the more he enjoys it. He built his first boat, a Heron dinghy, in 1960 and launched it with some friends in Fenloe Lake, Newmarket-on-Fergus. They had many good sailing days on the Heron, but Seán found that when he sailed it on Lough Derg it was too slow so he went on to build a fast Catamaran with bright red sails. He had this boat at the time we married and it always sailed fast and sweetly, but not a toe would I put in it, except when it was out of the water.

A later boat, a sailing day cruiser called *Whimbrel* gave him great pleasure indeed, as he sailed at his ease between Ballyvaug-

Fenloe Lake

han and Galway. Retired from teaching, he could relax now and let the wind and the sails take him skimming over the sea.

Swimming in the Gaeltacht

The pier in Scariff

Getting Ready

I suppose preparations for Christmas, when I was a child, really began the first week of December, though we young people had been talking about it, planning for it and writing to Santy, long before this. Excitement grew though, when mothers busily cleaned and painted any room that needed a facelift before 25 December, especially if visitors from England or farther afield were coming for the holiday.

We never had visitors staying over at this time of year as a rule. Just once though, our maternal grandmother came to care for and indeed spoil us for the Christmas, following the birth of our sister Ena who arrived on 21 December – the shortest day of the year!

Ena's arrival was a complete surprise to Sheelagh and me and for me it was almost like having a baby of my own, and at Christmas times too – the wonder of it! I took a real fancy to Ena from the beginning and this has not changed over the years. Having our beloved Granny with us for Christmas, for whatever reason, was a real novelty and must have been a great help to Mam.

We were fascinated by chimney sweeps. They were very busy in the few weeks before the holiday because of the big fires needed to heat our houses during seriously cold spells of weather, and because of the usual use of fires in the sitting-room during the holiday. These fireplaces were rarely used during the rest of the year and birds' nests could have lodged in them. We were always very relieved when our chimney was cleaned, because we wanted to be quite sure that Santy could come safely and cleanly into our room where the stockings were hanging in wait for him. On a small table nearby, a glass of sherry and a piece of rich, fruity Christmas cake – to help him on his journey.

We never saw any soot around on Christmas morning, so we felt that the chimney sweep must have been very good at his job. Also, Santy never left any sherry or crumbs after him either and we were always glad of this.

Christmas Markets

The Christmas markets, held every week for a few weeks beforehand, were very busy and particularly the market which was held during Christmas week. The bird, for what we felt was the most important meal of the year, would be booked already, paid for, and then taken home from this last market. As I remember it, one had to be very careful moving around sculleries or back hallways in the dark. Remember I am talking of that special time before electricity. The bird, complete with feathers, would be hung up from a piece of twine tied around its feet and I can tell you it was scary indeed to walk quickly into one of these – especially late at night. I remember it well, I had many such frights and so too had my friends.

Drinks for the season were bought in advance too, and kept in the sideboard in the sitting-room. We usually bought one bottle of sherry and port, a dozen of lemonade and orange squash and a dozen bottles of porter. When all this was in the house we felt ready for callers and one step nearer to Christmas.

But, when O'Shea's lifted the blind on their shop window in early December to reveal, to us, a wonderland of toys, woolly hats, scarves and gloves, Christmas had indeed arrived.

Worrying about Christmas!

Skating to My Heart

December's icy fingers weave a fine lace tracery on the window-panes today. I find that in the frozen air my breath flows prettily in front of me as if playing a game. Now, winter has cast her spell over the countryside, leaving dykes and lakes deeply frozen.

I was coming up to my eighth Christmas when we had extremely cold, frosty weather, beginning before we got our holidays from school, and of course, setting a hope in our hearts that we would have snow. The cold spell lasted for many weeks after the holiday, but the snow did not come at all. It was real chilblain-stinging weather and yet we gloried in the crispness and were happy we did not have rain. And at night time, before we pulled the blind in our bedroom, we stood in the cold, gazing at the starry sky and trying to decide which one might be the Christmas star. Maybe if we were lucky we might see movement up there, indeed if we were very attentive we might see the face of the baby Jesus shining down from above on us alone. If it were not for the cold, we would probably gaze longer and later, but usually the frozen toes, fingers and nose, coaxed us to our beds.

But oh, what fun in the school-yard though, breaking the ice on the little pools of surface water – like breaking glass. And sometimes on the way home from school, trying to smash, with the heel of our strong boots, the larger frozen puddles outside Furlong's and Jones'. But how we would love to have the courage to skate if we were only just a little older.

We had a slight slope in the road, beginning outside our house and from about, let's say, the second frosty night, a 'respectable' slide began there and you could increase the speed with each metre, and get quite a good speed going towards the Feakle road. One particular evening we were doing our lessons by the range, and Dad was reading the paper before going back to do duty in the garda barracks, when Mam came in with a can of milk that she had bought in Flannery's across the road. Peeling off the cloths that she had wound around her shoes, to prevent herself slipping, she declared: 'That does it, you'll have to talk to Seán Dinan about that slide before someone breaks a leg. He always starts the slide and that's a fact, I saw himself yesterday'.

'Asha, he is a nice young lad all the same, tall for his age too,' came from behind the paper.

'Tall or not, have a word with him tomorrow or I won't be able to get out to do my Christmas shopping!'

Little did she think then, that some years later, the young skater would become her much-loved son-in-law.

Isn't he a handsome snowman!

Caught in the snow near Cappabane, Scariff, in February in 1933

Fruit, Spices and Chocolate!

We did our main shopping at Mrs Phelan's and though we gave our custom, as it were, to other shops near us, Phelan's was where we got our weekly groceries. The items were written in to a small red passbook and at the end of each month, Mrs Phelan totted it up and we paid what was due.

I was the shopper, mostly. Mam did the visit each time to settle our account. Once, when Sheelagh was in hospital having her appendix out, Ena, who was just coming up to four years at the time, brought the red passbook to Mrs Phelan and then requested a box of chocolate for her sister who was sick. Fortunately, Mrs Phelan was uneasy about the unusual request, so she checked with Mam, but not before Ena had eaten five three-penny bars!

Saturday was my favourite shopping day. Chores over, I was ready for Phelan's. I was always warmly greeted and as Saturday was a very busy day in the shop, she would usually ask if I would be so good as to wait – or was I maybe in a hurry? I never said I was in a hurry because I loved being in the shop, especially in winter and particularly coming up to Christmas.

The place smelled of fruit, tea and spices, especially cinnamon. It smelled too of soap, newspapers and the welcome smell of the oil stove that sat outside the counter for the benefit of the customers. Sitting on a low stool near the stove, I watched the proceedings. It amazed me the amount of goods bought by some, especially those from out the country who were not close to a shop.

The chocolate person in the centre of Sheelagh and myself

Mrs Phelan was gentle and warm-hearted. She had on-going conversations as she weighed and packed tea and sugar, fruit for baking, flour, butter, spices and jams. Tinned peas and beans were very popular, as were cooked breakfasts and teas. So, sausages, puddings and tomatoes were weighed and wrapped and there was room in the

Outside May Coffey's shop

box too for lemonade and biscuits and at Christmas time, a box of chocolates.

I loved the ambience and would happily stay all afternoon in the warmth and in a dream, as it were, if she didn't bring me out of my reverie with: 'You're a patient child, Colette, and thank you for sitting so quietly.' This lifted my heart, as did the gift of a bar of chocolate which usually came my way.

Always during Christmas week, she wrote a list of half a dozen or so items, and then I had to run and show it to Mam. They were things like a china tea-pot, a half set of delft, cutlery, a large jug with a nice rose pattern on the side, matching sugar and butter dishes or a shining aluminium saucepan! Mam would then choose one of the gifts and I would be dispatched back and forth, such excitement! And a nice practical present too.

When the shop shelves were laden with goodies of every description, and when the cotton wool sat thickly amid the tinsel on the decorated window, my imagination ran riot and my friends felt the same. The growing excitement was occasionally tinged with fear, as we wondered if we had been good enough for Santy to come. Though I knew how hard I had tried, there was always a small worry there until Christmas morning. Then, what a blessed feeling of relief and euphoria – Santy never let us down!

Decorations, Candles, Excitement

Mam always made one Christmas cake, and we bought the pudding. Our neighbour, Mrs Cunneen, made several cakes and puddings and we were allowed to help her each year. She let us lick the bowl afterwards and we left it spotless after us.

Chopping peel, removing stones from raisins, and busily grating nutmeg, apples, orange and lemon rind just increased the excitement and made us giggly and giddy too. To be honest, Mrs Cunneen would probably have worked faster without our help, but for us, it was special to be included, and she did enjoy our chatter.

In our early years, Christmas cards were a great novelty and much treasured. Presents, however, were not exchanged at all – we had not the money to spare for presents and nor had any of our friends. Just the same, we were very occupied with Christmas. For instance, we took our Christmas choir very seriously, and worked hard in an unheated church, rehearsing and practising and we always felt that it was worth it all.

We were well aware, at the Christmas Mass, that we had given joy to the listeners and to the 'family in the crib'. I was always convinced that the group in the crib enjoyed our choir and that they had a chat together when we had gone home.

On Christmas Eve the candle was decorated, the lino on the stairs and landing polished. We carefully pinned up the decorations that we and our friends had laboured over, on many an evening. Inch-wide strips of red and green crêpe paper were folded in such a way that it opened out concertina-fashion and we pinned it about the rooms so that it hung in loops – we felt that this just suited the occasion. Fresh holly sprigs were placed on every available window ledge and over each door. The precious cards were carefully arranged on the mantel-piece in the sitting-room where we would spend Christmas day, and each day of the holiday, toasting ourselves in front of a huge turf fire – turf cut and saved by Dad.

Nora and Kathleen, right next door, had the most beautifully decorated candle in the town. We, the children from nearby anyway, gathered for what was like a ritual each year. The gold decorations, for we were sure they were gold, were taken carefully from their box by Nora and placed in the same order each year while we looked on in awe. Then there was the lighting of the candle and the placing of the beautiful tiny wax figure of the baby Jesus in front of the candle.

In our home, when the candle was lit and the Holy Water sprinkled, it was seriously Christmas now, and time to hang up the stockings!

Out of doors what a spectacle! What magic! Lights from the candles at the windows making a glow on to the streets and painting a Christmas card scene

to a drab December evening. And if you went upstairs, and looked up the countryside – well a myriad of candlelights twinkled and winked back at you. What bliss!

We were sent to bed earlier than usual on Christmas Eve, I suppose to give the adults a bit of peace from the 'what-ifs?' – 'what if Santy doesn't come?', etc. We were scrubbed extra clean and there was a sense of great occasion and we quietly sat when we were asked. On other nights, when the fire was so inviting that we were lazy to move, we would try every way we could to delay going up-stairs. But, when Mam called out 'no more delaying tactics now, and off to bed straight away' – we knew it was time to go. However, Christmas Eve was different and we were positively angelic.

Because I was a few years older, I managed to stay awake after Sheelagh and Ena had fallen asleep – indeed I could not sleep anyway if I tried. When the house was quiet, I would steal out to the landing window, as it did not have a blind, it just had three pots of geraniums on the window ledge. I hated the smell of geraniums actually, but on a night such as this, I was unaware of anything unpleasant as I watched and waited for Santy, on the eve of the birth of Jesus. As I became colder, I heard Dad in the hallway telling Mam in a loud whisper 'I just spotted Santy and his reindeer coming smoothly over Flannery's, he'll be here any minute now.'

I was in bed, head covered, before you could say 'Christmas' and asleep immediately from the warmth of the bed, sheer exhaustion, and the relief that Santy had managed to travel with all that frost around.

Christmas Day

Making our way to Mass on Christmas morning to our church on the hill, in the half dark, felt strange and somehow impressive. As we strode out our front door and crossed the road to the green, by May Coffey's and Flannery's, we were joined by the Cunneens coming from our right and Nora and Kathleen from our left, followed by Guard and Mrs Corcoran and their family. As we crossed the green, it seemed as if there were people coming in huge numbers from every direction, and this before seven in the morning. Do you know what we often noticed too? Country people were always in early and they probably had miles to walk.

Funnily enough, I do not ever remember rain on the way to this, the first Mass of Christmas day; but I do remember the frost and I can still taste the cold. However, the moon and stars lighted our way and added an element of glamour, as if we were not walking on air already.

When we caught up with the Longs, and some of our schoolfriends, we ran ahead up the hill and arrived breathless at the church door. We were dressed in our best Christmas finery and were eager to meet everyone, but because we were not allowed to see the crib until after Mass, we made our way upstairs to

the choir gallery. Up there, we had the thrill of a few quick words with each other – comparing notes on what Santy had bought. We got many of the same things, dolls, paints, oranges and books, but the whispering among us was soon quietened down with a 'shush, shush, get out the hymn books and pay attention!'

From early on, we had a four-part choir, and a very good one too – even if I say so myself. Mam was a choir member then, so we were brought along from the time we could walk. I would feel very strange now if I were not in a choir, especially at Christmas. The first Mass of Christmas was always crowded and everyone tried to come if they could at all. Mind you, before churches were heated, you either dressed warmly or you could not sing with the cold.

After we had visited the crib, it was time to run home, and enjoy our Santy presents again and at our leisure. Fingers of light were always coming up in the sky as we came out from Mass, and the light invariably took us by surprise.

Nobody drove to Mass in those days, cars were very rare, anyway. As well as that, we were young and active and would not want to miss the walk. This walk was part of our Christmas tradition and we found the early morning buzz, of meeting friends, fascinating and rewarding.

Christmas dinner, which we usually had around two o'clock in the afternoon,  was a real feast. Goose was what we ate and what was eaten in the homes of our friends and neighbours. Turkeys were scarce then and quite expensive – and now it is the reverse isn't it? With the goose we had tasty stuffing, carrots and parsnips, baked and roast potatoes and steepy peas. The dessert was always a nice boozy trifle and then plum pudding with iced cake to follow – if we had room for it. Such luxury! We children carried the delft out to the scullery afterwards. We washed up, tidied, and ran quickly back to the warmth of the sitting-room. We sat lazily around the fire, occasionally glancing through any books we may have been given, and dreamily looking at the pictures, formed by the turf, as it burned.

Mam usually had a sherry in the late afternoon, Dad had mulled porter and we had lemonade, biscuits, some sweets and maybe an orange as well.

When the Cunneens, the Longs and Corcorans came, we were more than ready for 'blind man's buff' in the kitchen, but first Dad would play favourite tunes on the melodeon. We all joined in and sang with gusto and when the music moved on to something more lively, we young ones would run with our friends to the kitchen where we danced and giggled and generally enjoyed just being together. The sheer contentment and happiness that we felt as a group on such occasions makes me very glad indeed that we lived through times of simple pleasures and home entertainment. The games went on far into the evening and though Sheelagh was young, she was great to think up games. Ena always escaped being caught in 'blind man's buff', because in the time I am telling about, she was young and very tiny. But we did trip over her many times and she never cried. If the noise, if you like, from the games lessened, or if we were quiet at all, Mam would call out: 'What trick-acting are ye at out there?' and we always answered by giggling uncontrollably.

When the friends returned to their homes, and of course we always escorted them the short distance, we returned to the sitting-room and sat around the fire. Mam made our evening cocoa for us and then we simply chatted until they began to tell stories of their young days and Christmases past, and things they had done and seen. A sing-song always began again, and when we had once more done our party pieces, Mam would sing 'Galway Bay' and 'Teddy O'Neill'. And when he had sung 'Danny Boy' and 'The Banks', Dad would settle himself back in his armchair, and with great feeling and from the heart, would sing 'Bendimeer Stream'.

We will never know now what special happy memories it evoked for him, but he had a softness about his face when he sang and tears glistened in his eyes. Song over, he closed his eyes and he was always quiet for minutes afterwards, and so were we.

We had a great sense of occasion and of course, we had had a very busy, tiring and fulfilled day.

The New Year

On St Stephen's day Kathleen and Nora went to visit their brother in Dromad, Bodyke and we were lost without them! In the afternoon of St Stephen's day, when the 'wranboys' became plentiful it helped to make us forget about our missing neighbours. By the time the adults, and we always called them the 'big wranboys', came around it was almost time for our friends to return to their home and back to us, laden with goodies and very happy always with their visit. The 'big wranboys', though well disguised, were known to us, and we were usually able to tell who they were – sometimes by their walk or even their hands. They always brought music with them and danced and sang and gave a good account of themselves. Naturally, dozens of children trailed along and escorted the party from door to door. Some homes had large kitchens to the front and the group had much fun and music in these places. We were content to wait outside and because we could clearly hear, we felt part of the hilarity going on inside.

New Year's Eve was the next big event, though in between, we had much fun in each other's homes. In Scariff, there was always a bonfire between the market house and the green. When darkness fell, we could hardly wait for the music and dance around the fire to begin. My early memory of New Year's Eve is hazy enough even though we could see the big fire and the bright red sparks flying up from it, from a front bedroom, and we could hear the music and the sound of merriment. With the light from the glowing fire brightening the square, we were able to identify most of the dancers too. Of course, when we were older, we were out there with the rest – to the very end.

When we all joined hands and sang 'Auld Lang Syne' it was time to return home to our parents who were watching and waiting for us. Dad was some times with us if he was on duty, either way, he always 'first footed'. By tradition, the first person to enter a house at New Year should be tall and dark-haired. If I were outside after midnight, Mam would not let me, with my red hair, inside the door until someone with black hair had been in first to say 'A happy New Year and good luck to all here'.

Those were the days, indeed they were.